Secrets Of Credit Card Processing Fees Revealed

By Gingergaye Hollowell

Secrets of Credit Card Processing Revealed
www.ElectronicMoneyCompany.com

Copyright © 2014 by Gingergaye Hollowell

All rights reserved. No part of this publication may be reproduced, distributed, or transmitted in any form or by any means, including photocopying, recording, or other electronic or mechanical methods, without the prior written permission of the publisher, except in the case of brief quotations embodied in critical reviews and certain other noncommercial uses permitted by copyright law. For permission requests, write to the publisher or author.

ISBN-13: 978-15025840-3-8
ISBN-10: 1502584034

Published by:
Gingergaye Hollowell
www.ElectronicMoneyCompany.com

Edited by:
Jennifer-Crystal Johnson
www.JenniferCrystalJohnson.com

Disclaimer:

Although the author and publisher have made every effort to ensure that the information in this book was correct at press time, the author and publisher do not assume and hereby disclaim any liability to any party for any loss, damage, or disruption caused by errors or omissions, whether such errors or omissions result from negligence, accident, or any other cause.

Dedication

I dedicate this book to my children (all eight of you), to my grandchildren, and to my future grandchildren. I entered the work force when my baby, Casey, was three, kicking and screaming because I had to leave and go to work. I discovered that it was fun to be with adults. I discovered that I could help so many entrepreneurs and business people save money on their credit card processing. I discovered that I could get paid to talk to people and that it was so much fun and very fulfilling. Now I nurture my clients as I have and will continue to nurture my children.

Since you are all raised and I am so proud of who you have become, my new goal is to be an example of success to *you* as well as to my clients, friends, and all I meet. All of you have the power to create whatever you want. So go forth and think positively, appreciate your blessings, and vibrate happiness in your present moments… and you will call forth to you all that you desire. The world will be a better place because of it.

And I dedicate this book to my husband, Walt, who has always been, and always will be, the feet beneath my wings. My heart and soul thanks you and appreciates you.

Acknowledgements

I would like to acknowledge all my clients who continue to trust that I have their best interests at heart, and to all my clients who have referred many multiples of other clients. I appreciate your business and your referrals.

I would also like to acknowledge the special people with whom I work directly at the home office processor. Your support, teaching, and endless question-answering in this ever-changing industry have given me the opportunity to support our shared clients.

Table Of Contents

Introduction	7
Chapter One	
The History of Credit Card Processing	9
Chapter Two	
Why Should I Even Take Credit Cards In My Business?	13
Chapter Three	
How Are My Merchant Fees Determined?	19
Chapter Four	
The So-Called "Hidden Fees"	57
Chapter Five	
General Guidelines By Industry	61
Chapter Six	
Value Added Services	67
Chapter Seven	
Summary	73
Bonus Chapter	
Bloody Stories Dealing With Bob From Brand X	77
A Personal Afterword	93
Addendum C	95
What Merchant Clients Are Saying About Electronic Money Company	97

Secrets of Credit Card Processing Revealed
www.ElectronicMoneyCompany.com

Gingergaye Hollowell
www.ElectronicMoneyCompany.com

Introduction

Credit card processing fees are complex and confusing. Trying to understand them is like balancing on a tightrope while spinning a bunch of plates. It's not your fault. I wrote this book to get you off the tightrope and reduce the number of spinning plates to give you the upper hand in negotiating against the sleazy credit card processing salesperson. Let's give him a name: Bob from Brand X. Let's even give him the benefit of the doubt and assume he is not trying to be sleazy, but is cluelessly playing through a script written by his processing company.

This book is intended to educate business owners. I have run across owners, accountants, GMs, and even CEOs who tell me they just got an offer to save them however many dollars on their credit card processing. It looks good, but they don't know how to confirm the analysis on their own without the correct knowledge and understanding of the complicated rate structure of payment processing. And these are smart people. Most often, Bob from Brand X has plugged his calculations with assumptions. The merchant is swayed by the lure of big savings, switches processors, and then, lo and behold, his rates went higher. He did his due diligence and analyzed Bob's numbers but still ended up worse off than when he started, and in addition, is now beat up from the experience.

What happened? How are so many people getting duped? Better yet, how does a business person get on the topside of the credit card processing fee analysis? The answer to that question is inside this book. The only solution is to get the straight scoop and gain a basic understanding of where the numbers come from and how the fees are calculated.

The most important question is how to separate the wholesale cost of processing from the processor's service fee on top of the wholesale cost.

Here is my depiction of Bob.

Bob from Brand X

And inside this book is how to beat him at his game!

Chapter One

The History Of Credit Card Processing

I think that it is important to understand why there are credit card processing fees in the first place, along with some background on why and how credit card processing was created and its purpose and value.

1914 – It all started with Western Union, who created a metal card with deferred payment for preferred customers at a specific store or group of stores owned by the same company.

This practice of only being able to use the card at the store where it was issued lasted until World War II, when all credit and charge cards became prohibited. The practice changed after the war and these Western Union cards became quite prominent, especially in the travel industry because of people's need to have access to larger sums of money without the risk of carrying so much cash.

1946 – John Biggins created the "charge-it" card. You could use the card to make purchases at more than one local store. The merchants got the authorization from the bank before the customer left the store. Biggins Bank collected from the customer and reimbursed the merchants, while keeping a fee for the transaction.

Other banks wanted to join in the opportunity.

1950 - A man named Frank McNamara had a business dinner in New York. When the bill arrived, he realized he had forgotten his wallet. He convinced the restaurant that he would return to pay, but then and there he decided there should be an alternative to cash. He created the Diner's Club card which was created as a "Travel & Entertainment Card." It allowed 60 days for the customer to settle. Diner's Club became the first "acquirer" because they were the first to charge the merchant a "discount fee." Understand that there is no discount. The "discount fee" is in reality an interest charge for the money the bank was advancing to the merchant. It also covered the missing revenue from loans that could have been given to consumers. By 1951, there were 20,000 Diner's Club cards in circulation.

1958 – American Express created their own T & E card. They had previously specialized in money orders and traveler's checks. They didn't want to be outdone by Diner's. They eventually introduced the first card made of plastic. American Express also introduced their card to other countries. Within five years, they had a million cards in circulation.

Also in 1958, Bank of America in California allowed customers to carry debt on their cards and to make monthly payments to settle their debt on their T & E cards. The merchant got charged the "discount fee" and the customer got charged an interest rate to carry the debt. At the same time, Bank of America realized that their labor costs went down compared to handling cash and checks. So the card industry was profitable from three angles: for the merchant, the consumer, *and* the savings of overhead. Their card was known as the BankAmericard.

1960 – Bank of America issued licenses to other banks outside of California for the privilege of issuing the BankAmericard to their customers. The banks exchanged information with each other regarding card transactions. This later became known as "interchange." Today, all banks pay each other "interchange fees" when a card transaction takes place. It is the bank who issued the card to the consumer who earns the bulk of the fees paid by the merchant accepting the card. For example, if you go into Macy's and purchase with a credit card issued by Bank of America, then Bank of America gets the "interchange,"

11

the bulk of the "discount rate" paid by the merchant. If you have a credit card issued by Wells Fargo, then Wells Fargo gets the interchange.

1966 – 14 banks met in NY to form the Interbank Card Association (ICA). They formed this association to compete with the BankAmericard. They agreed to exchange credit card information with each other. They established rules for authorizing, clearing, and settlement. They shared marketing strategies, security, and legal information.

1966 – The UK launched their first card, the Barclay Card.

1967 – Four banks in California formed Western United States Bankcard Association and branded it MasterCharge. They later licensed with the Interbank Card Association to continue using the same name.

1970 – Electronics allowed for 24 hour settlement.

1976 – BankAmericard changed their name to VISA USA.

Chapter Two

Why Should I Even Take Credit Cards In My Business?

More Sales

First of all, you close more sales when you take plastic. Why would you *not* want to accept your customers' money any way they want to give it to you? The card gives the customer more buying power and more money to spend than what they are limited to by their checking account or the amount of cash in their pocket.

Remember from chapter one that credit cards originated from the idea that money and the economy can expand. The whole concept of loans is to expand the economy and that means your customer's personal economy as well as your economy. If kids had to wait until they had college tuition in hand, there would be far fewer kids going to college and therefore far fewer people growing the economy with their knowledge. I'll bet you know your own spending habits inside your family. Did you purchase a house with a mortgage? Don't you and your spouse spend more on your credit card than what is currently available in your pocket?

Customer Comfort

Second, people don't carry much cash anymore. Customers carry a debit card, a credit card, or both. They do not carry a checkbook because it is bulky and they do not carry cash because it's risky to carry a lot of cash. There's no need to carry cash when you have a debit or credit card. By accepting credit cards, you reduce the risk of losing a sale. You don't want to send them out the door to go get cash or their checkbook because they will most likely *not* return.

Immediate Sales

Thirdly, close the sale *now*.

You believe in your product and you believe your customers will better themselves by purchasing your product. You want to close the sale now without risking the chance of your customer not coming back. The statistics are that if you don't close the sale now, you only have a 10% chance that the customer will return and buy later. Plus, not taking plastic is like telling someone to go shop with your competitor who is happy to take your customer's money via a credit card.

So, the fact is that people spend more *and* more often with plastic. Don't miss that boat! Don't stop your customers from spending more money in your business.

Some merchants get concerned about the cost of taking credit cards. But many times, it only takes one or two sales to cover the fees for all your customers! That's leverage. Simply figure in the processing fees as overhead.

Not Accepting Cards Costs You Money

Fourth, there is a cost if you don't take credit cards. People carry credit and debit cards because it is more convenient than carrying cash or their checkbook. They don't have to worry about losing cash or having it stolen. And by the way, neither do you. There is actually a cost to handling cash at your place of business. It can walk off, get lost, or get stolen. Have you noticed how airline stewardesses only take plastic now for drinks and snacks on flights? The airlines figured out that they make more profits paying credit card fees than they did with disappearing cash and lost sales from people not having enough cash with them.

Some merchants inappropriately think that it is less expensive to take checks than credit cards, that there is no cost to taking checks. Not so! First, a certain percentage of checks will bounce. Low or high, the percentage still exists. Second, it takes longer for a check to clear. Time is money. If that cash was sitting the bank, it would be earning interest for those days waiting on checks to clear. The loss of that interest is a cost of taking checks. Third, it costs money to pay someone to handle the paper check, mark it deposited on the books, and drive it to the bank. Some owners say there is no cost if they do it themselves. But that's like saying your time is not worth anything. Certainly you would like to be paid more than $0 for your efforts.

Customer Convenience

Fifth, convenience to customers is a big reason to take credit cards. Why not take the customer's money any way they want to spend it? The more you please your customers, the happier they are and the happier you are. Many professionals carry corporate credit cards for their expense account; as an example, to take clients to a restaurant. Without the ability to accept payment through their corporate card, you turn away not only *your* customers' business, but also the extra business from his clients. Taking credit cards is a great way to increase sales.

Faster Transactions

Sixth, you get paid faster.

Another reason to take credit cards in your business is that you get paid faster. Transactions are deposited daily and the funds are available sometimes as fast as the next morning. Again, that is much faster than handling checks or cash.

Time and convenience are money. The speed of money has a huge value. Instead of making an invoice, giving a customer 30 days to pay the invoice, and waiting for them to mail you a check, you get paid immediately. With checks you also have to deposit them and wait for them to clear. All this can be shortened by accepting credit cards. Get money now. Earn 30 days of interest or value and reinvest that money in your own business.

Building Trust

Finally, accepting credit cards allows your customer to trust in you. It says, "We are a thriving business!" It says, "If we do not live up to your standards, you can cancel your charge with your credit card company." Trust is a major reason for a customer to choose to do business with a particular merchant. Let's take the example of a contractor. Taking plastic tells his customers that he stands behind his product and service. If his client isn't happy, he can charge back the card.

Chapter Three

How Are My Merchant Fees Determined?

In theory, there are two overriding determinations of the fees for accepting credit cards: the **interchange cost** and the **processor's surcharge**.

1. **The interchange cost**. This is the fee the merchant pays to the issuing bank, the bank that issued the card to the customer and is handling the risk of loaning the money to the customer.
2. **The processor's surcharge** on top of the interchange fee. The processor services the merchant, checking for fraud, transferring money from the card to the merchant's bank account, and providing customer service such as troubleshooting equipment hiccups, questions about transaction deposits, questions about fees, or service requests such as address changes or bank account changes.

The processor surcharge can be negotiated with the processor via the credit card processing salesperson. The interchange cost can be controlled to some degree by the merchant as well. Let's tackle the details of interchange cost first.

Interchange Cost

(See Figure A)

As you can see, there are many categories of rates. It is a complicated system. Every October and April, the bank association gets together and decides if they are collecting enough of a percentage on each category to cover their risk for that category. As there are changes, the processors individually need to evaluate if their surcharge fees cover any increases or if their surcharge needs to be adjusted. I will talk more about this later in the detailed section regarding processor fees.

Percentage Rate and Transaction Fee

The cost of credit card processing includes both a percentage rate and a transaction fee. Remember that the issuing banks are earning by far the largest portion of the cost of processing. They are in effect charging an interest fee for the loan they are giving your customers and therefore the credit they are offering you to give to your customers. If they charged only a percentage rate, they could not make a fair rate of return on a $5.00 charge. If they charged only a transaction fee, they could not make a fair return for the risk on a $5,000 charge. Therefore, they combine a percentage rate and a transaction fee.

Secrets of Credit Card Processing Revealed
www.ElectronicMoneyCompany.com

Figure A

INTERCHANGE

This Interchange Rate Schedule contains a summary of the primary qualification criteria established by Visa®, Master inclusive. In the event of any ambiguity or conflict, the interchange requirements established by the Card Organization For a complete list, call the number on your merchant statement. Please note that Discover Network fees apply only to and fees, please call Customer Service.

Program Rate Category	Rates		
	Fee Per Sales $	Per Item	
VISA			
CPS / Retail Credit	1.51%	$0.10	Consumer Traditional Cards. Card Present / Magnetic Stripe Read / Sign number and check-in / check-out dates required. For Passenger Transport service category 1, ancillary ticket document number, issued in connectic
CPS / Retail Debit	0.80%	$0.15	indicators. Authorization and settlement amount on check card transactic Shops - 7230, Health and Beauty Spas - 7298). Supermarkets (5411), Ser
CPS / Retail Prepaid	1.15%	$0.15	prepaid transactions at Hotels (3501-3999, 7011), Car Rental (3351-3441 not eligible for this program. Maximum 2 days to deposit & settle.
Regulated Debit	0.05%	$0.22	Regulated Consumer Debit and Prepaid, Business Debit, and Commercia Card interchange. Authorization required. CPS requirements recommend Debit program are not eligible for this program. Maximum 30 days to de
CPS / Restaurant Credit	1.54%	$0.10	
CPS / Restaurant Debit	1.19%	$0.10	Consumer Traditional Cards. Same requirements as CPS/Retail. Authori
CPS / Restaurant Prepaid	1.15%	$0.15	of auth date. Eligible Merchants: Restaurants (5812) and Fast Food Rest
CPS / Rewards 1	1.65%	$0.10	Consumer Traditional Rewards card that meet existing requirements for 4722, 5812, 5814, 7011, 7512). Visa Signature cards at merchants that p
CPS / Rewards 2	1.95%	$0.10	Consumer Traditional Rewards card that meet existing requirements for Transport, CPS/Hotel & Car Rental: Card Present / Card Not Present, an Entry, and CPS/E-Commerce Basic by non-Travel Services merchants (
CPS / Small Ticket Credit	1.65%	$0.04	Traditional, Traditional Rewards, Signature and Infinite consumer cards Federal Reserve final rule on Debit Card interchange are eligible for the
CPS / Small Ticket Debit	1.55%	$0.04	transactions must include bill payment indicators. Purchase date must be Dispensers (5542), Direct Marketing - Insurance (5960), Direct Marketin Marketing - Outbound Telemarketing (5966), Direct Marketing - Inboun
CPS / Small Ticket Prepaid	1.60%	$0.05	Automated Cash (6011), Financial Institutions - Merchandise & Service (9752), and Intra-Company Purchases (9950). Transaction amount must Threshold (Tier) MVV interchange programs are eligible for this progra
CPS / Small Ticket Debit Regulated	0.05%	$0.22	Debit Tax Payment. Maximum 2 days to deposit & settle.
CPS / Retail Key Entered Credit	1.80%	$0.10	Consumer Traditional Cards. Key-Entered due to inability to read magn positive match on Zip Code or full address. For hotel and car rental (330
CPS / Retail Key Entered Debit	1.65%	$0.15	4112, 4511); ticket number and itinerary required; transactions that inclu name) are not eligible for this program. Bill payment transactions must i
CPS / Retail Key Entered Prepaid	1.75%	$0.20	5964-5969), Cardholder Activated Terminal merchants are not eligible f
CPS / Card Not Present Credit	1.80%	$0.10	Consumer Traditional Cards. Card Not Present / Signature Not Obtained 8049, 8050, 8062, 8071, 8099), Emerging Market (9211, 9222, 9399, 82
CPS / Card Not Present Debit	1.65%	$0.15	invoice / order number required. Authorization required. Purchase date
CPS / Card Not Present Prepaid	1.75%	$0.20	payment indicators. Maximum 2 days to deposit & settle.
CPS / E-Commerce Basic Credit	1.80%	$0.10	Consumer Traditional Cards. Same requirements as CPS/Card Not Pres Market (9211, 9222, 9399, 8211, 8220, 8299, 5960, 6300, 4899, 4814, 6
CPS / E-Commerce Basic Debit	1.65%	$0.15	payment transactions must include bill payment indicators. Purchase dat
CPS / E-Commerce Basic Prepaid	1.75%	$0.20	Aggregation transactions must not exceed $15.00. Maximum 2 days to c
CPS / E-Commerce Preferred Credit	1.80%	$0.10	
CPS / E-Commerce Preferred Debit	1.60%	$0.15	Traditional, Traditional Rewards, Signature and Infinite consumer cards Verified by Visa. Maximum 2 days to deposit & settle.
CPS / E-Comm Preferred Prepaid	1.75%	$0.20	

Gingergaye Hollowell
www.ElectronicMoneyCompany.com

RATE SCHEDULE   (Effective April, 2014)

Card®, and Discover® Network (sometimes referred to as Discover) for most interchange programs - it is not all
s (sometimes referred to as associations) will determine the interchange programs at which your transactions qualify.
Discover transactions acquired by Bank of America Merchant Services. For more information regarding your Rates

Transaction Qualification Information

ature Obtained / Authorized. Purchase date must be within 1 day of auth date. For Hotel and Car Rental, Folio / Rental Agreement
: full itinerary required (including ticket number, passenger name, and trip leg data); transactions that include ancillary data (ancillary
on with ticket number, and passenger name) are not eligible for this program. Bill payment transactions must include bill payment
ns do not need to match for certain merchant segments (Taxis and Limousines - 4121, Bars and Taverns - 5813, Beauty and Barber
vice Stations (5541), Restaurants (5812, 5814), and High Risk (5962, 5966, 5967) not eligible for this program. Consumer debit and
, 7512), Passenger Transport (3000-3299, 4511, 4112), Cruise Lines / Steamships (4411), Travel Agencies & Tour Operators (4722)

d Prepaid Cards identified by Issuers and Card Organizations as being subject to the June 29, 2011 Federal Reserve final rule on Debit
led but not required. Regulated Consumer Debit and Prepaid transactions that meet qualifications for the CPS/Small Ticket Regulated
posit & settle.

zed amount does not have to match transaction amount. Authorization and magnetic stripe required. Purchase date must be within 1 day
aurants (5814). Maximum 2 days to deposit & settle.

CPS/Retail or CPS/Supermarket. Visa Signature and Infinite cards at non-Travel Services merchants (3000-3999, 4112, 4411, 4511,
articipate in the Retail or Supermarket Performance Threshold (Tier) MVV interchange programs. Maximum 2 days to deposit & settle.

CPS/Card Not Present, CPS/Retail Key Entry, or CPS/E-Commerce Basic, CPS/E-Commerce Preferred: Hotel/Car Rental & Passenger
d CPS/Passenger Transport and CPS/Restaurant. Signature and Infinite cards that meet existing CPS/Card Not Present, CPS/Retail Key
3000-3999, 4112, 4411, 4511, 4722, 5812, 5814, 7011, 7512). Maximum 2 days to deposit & settle.

. Regulated Consumer Debit and Prepaid Cards identified by Issuers and Card Organizations as being subject to the June 29, 2011
CPS/Small Ticket Regulated Debit rate. Card present / magnetic stripe read and authorized. Signature not required. Bill payment
within 1 day of auth date. Eligible Merchants include all merchants with the exception of: Money Transfer (4829), Automated Fuel
g - Travel Arrangement (5962), Direct Marketing - Catalog (5964), Direct Marketing - Combination Catalog & Retail (5965), Direct
d Telemarketing (5967), Direct Marketing - Continuity / Subscription (5968), Direct Marketing - Other (5969), Manual Cash (6010),
s (6012), Betting / Casinos / Race Tracks (7995), Intra-Government Purchases (9405), UK Supermarkets (9751), UK Petrol Stations
be less than or equal to $15.00. Small Ticket transactions from merchants that participate in Retail or Supermarket Performance
m. Small Ticket Credit eligible transactions will qualify for the following MVV interchange programs: Utilities, Debt Repayment, and

atic stripe. All requirements of CPS/Retail except magnetic stripe read. Authorization required. Address Verification Required with a
0-3799, 7011, 7512): Folio / Rental Agreement number and check-in / check-out dates required. For Passenger Transport (3000-3299,
ide ancillary data (ancillary service category 1, ancillary ticket document number, issued in connection with ticket number, and passenger
nclude bill payment indicators. Purchase date must be within 1 day of auth date. Automated Fuel (5542), Direct Marketing (5960, 5962,
or this program. Credit transactions at Quasi-Cash (6051) merchants not eligible for this program. Maximum 2 days to deposit & settle.

l / Mail or Phone Order. Address Verification required unless Healthcare (4119, 5975, 5976, 7277, 8011, 8021, 8031, 8041, 8042, 8043,
:11, 8220, 8299, 5960, 6300, 4899, 4814, 6513, 5968, 5983, 8351, 8398), or Utilities (4900). Customer Service phone number and
must be within 7 days of auth date. Authorization and settlement amounts must match. Bill payment transactions must include bill

ent but transaction takes place in a secure Internet environment. Authorization required. Address Verification required unless Emerging
(513, 5968, 5983, 8351, 8398), or Utilities (4900). E-Commerce requires additional data fields in authorization and settlement. Bill
e must be within 7 days of auth date (or within 3 days for Transaction Aggregation transactions). Authorization amount for Transaction
leposit & settle.

. Same requirements as E-Commerce Basic, except require Cardholder Authentication Value (CAVV). Authorization required. Requires

Secrets of Credit Card Processing Revealed
www.ElectronicMoneyCompany.com

INTERCHANGE

This Interchange Rate Schedule contains a summary of the primary qualification criteria established by Visa®, Master[...] inclusive. In the event of any ambiguity or conflict, the interchange requirements established by the Card Organization[...] For a complete list, call the number on your merchant statement. Please note that Discover Network fees apply only to[...] and fees, please call Customer Service.

Program Rate Category	Rates		Description
	Fee Per Sales $	Per Item	
VISA			
CPS / Retail Credit	1.51%	$0.10	Consumer Traditional Cards. Card Present / Magnetic Stripe Read / Sign number and check-in / check-out dates required. For Passenger Transpor service category 1, ancillary ticket document number, issued in connecti
CPS / Retail Debit	0.80%	$0.15	indicators. Authorization and settlement amount on check card transacti Shops - 7230, Health and Beauty Spas - 7298). Supermarkets (5411), Se prepaid transactions at Hotels (3501-3999, 7011), Car Rental (3351-344
CPS / Retail Prepaid	1.15%	$0.15	not eligible for this program. Maximum 2 days to deposit & settle.
Regulated Debit	0.05%	$0.22	Regulated Consumer Debit and Prepaid, Business Debit, and Commerci Card interchange. Authorization required. CPS requirements recommen Debit program are not eligible for this program. Maximum 30 days to de
CPS / Restaurant Credit	1.54%	$0.10	Consumer Traditional Cards. Same requirements as CPS/Retail. Author of auth date. Eligible Merchants: Restaurants (5812) and Fast Food Res
CPS / Restaurant Debit	1.19%	$0.10	
CPS / Restaurant Prepaid	1.15%	$0.15	
CPS / Rewards 1	1.65%	$0.10	Consumer Traditional Rewards card that meet existing requirements for 4722, 5812, 5814, 7011, 7512). Visa Signature cards at merchants that p
CPS / Rewards 2	1.95%	$0.10	Consumer Traditional Rewards card that meet existing requirements for Transport, CPS/Hotel & Car Rental: Card Present / Card Not Present, ar Entry, and CPS/E-Commerce Basic by non-Travel Services merchants (
CPS / Small Ticket Credit	1.65%	$0.04	Traditional, Traditional Rewards, Signature and Infinite consumer cards Federal Reserve final rule on Debit Card interchange are eligible for the transactions must include bill payment indicators. Purchase date must b
CPS / Small Ticket Debit	1.55%	$0.04	Dispensers (5542), Direct Marketing - Insurance (5960), Direct Marketi Marketing - Outbound Telemarketing (5966), Direct Marketing - Inbou
CPS / Small Ticket Prepaid	1.60%	$0.05	Automated Cash (6011), Financial Institutions - Merchandise & Service (9752), and Intra-Company Purchases (9950). Transaction amount must Threshold (Tier) MVV interchange programs are eligible for this progr
CPS / Small Ticket Debit Regulated	0.05%	$0.22	Debit Tax Payment. Maximum 2 days to deposit & settle.
CPS / Retail Key Entered Credit	1.80%	$0.10	Consumer Traditional Cards. Key-Entered due to inability to read magn positive match on Zip Code or full address. For hotel and car rental (33(
CPS / Retail Key Entered Debit	1.65%	$0.15	4112, 4511): ticket number and itinerary required; transactions that incl name) are not eligible for this program. Bill payment transactions must
CPS / Retail Key Entered Prepaid	1.75%	$0.20	5964-5969), Cardholder Activated Terminal merchants are not eligible
CPS / Card Not Present Credit	1.80%	$0.10	Consumer Traditional Cards. Card Not Present / Signature Not Obtaine 8049, 8050, 8062, 8071, 8099), Emerging Market (9211, 9222, 9399, 8.
CPS / Card Not Present Debit	1.65%	$0.15	invoice / order number required. Authorization required. Purchase date payment indicators. Maximum 2 days to deposit & settle.
CPS / Card Not Present Prepaid	1.75%	$0.20	
CPS / E-Commerce Basic Credit	1.80%	$0.10	Consumer Traditional Cards. Same requirements as CPS/Card Not Pres Market (9211, 9222, 9399, 8211, 8220, 8299, 5960, 6300, 4899,
CPS / E-Commerce Basic Debit	1.65%	$0.15	payment transactions must include bill payment indicators. Purchase da Aggregation transactions must not exceed $15.00. Maximum 2 days to
CPS / E-Commerce Basic Prepaid	1.75%	$0.20	
CPS / E-Commerce Preferred Credit	1.80%	$0.10	Traditional, Traditional Rewards, Signature and Infinite consumer card Verified by Visa. Maximum 2 days to deposit & settle.
CPS / E-Commerce Preferred Debit	1.60%	$0.15	
CPS / E-Comm Preferred Prepaid	1.75%	$0.20	

Gingergaye Hollowell
www.ElectronicMoneyCompany.com

RATE SCHEDULE (Effective April, 2014)

Card®, and Discover® Network (sometimes referred to as Discover) for most interchange programs - it is not all
s (sometimes referred to as associations) will determine the interchange programs at which your transactions qualify,
Discover transactions acquired by Bank of America Merchant Services. For more information regarding your Rates

Transaction Qualification Information

ature Obtained / Authorized. Purchase date must be within 1 day of auth date. For Hotel and Car Rental, Folio / Rental Agreement
: full itinerary required (including ticket number, passenger name, and trip leg data); transactions that include ancillary data (ancillary
on with ticket number, and passenger name) are not eligible for this program. Bill payment transactions must include bill payment
ons do not need to match for certain merchant segments (Taxis and Limousines - 4121, Bars and Taverns - 5813, Beauty and Barber
rvice Stations (5541), Restaurants (5812, 5814), and High Risk (5962, 5966, 5967) not eligible for this program. Consumer debit and
1, 7512), Passenger Transport (3000-3299, 4511, 4112), Cruise Lines / Steamships (4411), Travel Agencies & Tour Operators (4722)

al Prepaid Cards identified by Issuers and Card Organizations as being subject to the June 29, 2011 Federal Reserve final rule on Debit
ded but not required. Regulated Consumer Debit and Prepaid transactions that meet qualifications for the CPS/Small Ticket Regulated
:posit & settle.

ized amount does not have to match transaction amount. Authorization and magnetic stripe required. Purchase date must be within 1 day
aurants (5814). Maximum 2 days to deposit & settle.

CPS/Retail or CPS/Supermarket. Visa Signature and Infinite cards as non-Travel Services merchants (3000-3999, 4112, 4411, 4511,
articipate in the Retail or Supermarket Performance Threshold (Tier) MVV interchange programs. Maximum 2 days to deposit & settle.

CPS/Card Not Present, CPS/Retail Key Entry, or CPS/E-Commerce Basic, CPS/E-Commerce Preferred: Hotel/Car Rental & Passenger
d CPS/Passenger Transport and CPS/Restaurant. Signature and Infinite cards that meet existing CPS/Card Not Present, CPS/Retail Key
3000-3999, 4112, 4411, 4511, 4722, 5812, 5814, 7011, 7512). Maximum 2 days to deposit & settle.

: Regulated Consumer Debit and Prepaid Cards identified by Issuers and Card Organizations as being subject to the June 29, 2011
CPS/Small Ticket Regulated Debit rate. Card present / magnetic stripe read and authorized. Signature not required. Bill payment
e within 1 day of auth date. Eligible Merchants include all merchants with the exception of: Money Transfer (4829), Automated Fuel
ng - Travel Arrangement (5962), Direct Marketing - Catalog (5964), Direct Marketing - Combination Catalog & Retail (5965), Direct
d Telemarketing (5967), Direct Marketing - Continuity / Subscription (5968), Direct Marketing - Other (5969), Manual Cash (6010),
s (6012), Betting / Casinos / Race Tracks (7995), Intra-Government Purchases (9405), UK Supermarkets (9751), UK Petrol Stations
be less than or equal to $15.00. Small Ticket transactions from merchants that participate in Retail or Supermarket Performance
um. Small Ticket Credit eligible transactions will qualify for the following MVV interchange programs: Utilities, Debt Repayment, and

etic stripe. All requirements of CPS/Retail except magnetic stripe read. Authorization required. Address Verification Required with a
00-3799, 7011, 7512); Folio / Rental Agreement number and check-in / check-out dates required. For Passenger Transport (3000-3299,
ude ancillary data (ancillary service category 1, ancillary ticket document number, issued in connection with ticket number, and passenger
include bill payment indicators. Purchase date must be within 1 day of auth date. Automated Fuel (5542), Direct Marketing (5960, 5962,
for this program. Credit transactions at Quasi-Cash (6051) merchants not eligible for this program. Maximum 2 days to deposit & settle

d / Mail or Phone Order. Address Verification required unless Healthcare (4119, 59/5, 5976, 7277, 8011, 8021, 8031, 8041, 8042, 804
211, 8220, 8299, 5960, 6300, 4899, 4814, 6513, 5968, 5983, 8351, 8398), or Utilities (4900). Customer Service phone number and
must be within 7 days of auth date. Authorization and settlement amounts must match. Bill payment transactions must include bill

ent but transaction takes place in a secure Internet environment. Authorization required. Address Verification required unless Emerging
6513, 5968, 5983, 8351, 8398), or Utilities (4900). E-Commerce requires additional data fields in authorization and settlement. Bill
te must be within 7 days of auth date (or within 3 days for Transaction Aggregation transactions). Authorization amount for Transaction
deposit & settle.

s. Same requirements as E-Commerce Basic, except require Cardholder Authentication Value (CAVV). Authorization required. Require

Secrets of Credit Card Processing Revealed
www.ElectronicMoneyCompany.com

INTERCHANGE

Program Rate Category	Rates		
	Fee Per Sales $	Per Item	
CPS / Utilities Consumer	0.00%	$0.75	Traditional, Traditional Rewards, Signature, Infinite, Consumer Credit S requirements for CPS/Retail, CPS/Retail Key Entry, CPS/Small Ticket, that meet CPS/Retail, CPS/Retail Key Entry, or CPS/Small Ticket are no days to deposit & settle.
CPS / Utilities Cons Debit & Prepaid	0.00%	$0.65	
CPS / Utilities Business	0.00%	$1.50	
CPS / Utilities Bus Debit & Prepaid	0.00%	$1.50	
CPS / Account Funding Credit	2.14%	$0.10	Consumer Traditional, Rewards, and Signature card transactions to fund Card is not present. Full Address Verification Service (zip code and full Customer Service phone number, URL, or email address in authorization deposit & settle.
CPS / Account Funding Debit	1.75%	$0.20	
CPS / Account Funding Prepaid	1.80%	$0.20	
Electronic (EIRF) Credit and Signature Electronic	2.30%	$0.10	Key-Entered due to unreadable magnetic stripe and did not meet CPS/Re other CPS market specific requirements. For Passenger Transport (3000- data must be present (ancillary service category 1, ancillary ticket docum Transaction date is 3 days old. Bill payment transactions must include bi 4511), Passenger Railway (4112), Cruise Lines (4411), Lodging (3501-3 consumer debit and prepaid transactions and cap of $1.10 on consumer c
Electronic (EIRF) Debit	1.75%	$9.20	
Electronic (EIRF) Prepaid	1.80%	$0.20	
Debit Tax Payment	0.65%	$0.15	Consumer Debit and Prepaid cards that meet the existing requirements fo registration with Visa and MVV must be present. Purchase date must be of $2.00 on consumer debit and prepaid transactions. Maximum 2 days to
Debt Repayment	0.65%	$0.15	Consumer Debit and Prepaid cards that meet existing requirements for C must be present. Eligible Merchants: Financial Services-Merchandise an of $2.00 on consumer debit and prepaid transactions. Requires registrati
Signature Preferred Electronic	2.40%	$0.10	Signature Preferred and Consumer Credit Spend cards that meet existing 3999, 4112, 4411, 4511, 4722, 5812, 5814, 7011, 7512). Consumer Cred
Premium Consumer Credit Electronic	2.40%	$0.10	
Signature Preferred Retail	2.10%	$0.10	Signature Preferred and Consumer Credit Spend cards that meet existing 4411, 4511, 4722, 5812, 5814, 7011, 7512) merchants. Consumer Credit (8398) and Utilities (4900) not eligible for this program. Maximum 2 day
Premium Consumer Credit Retail	2.10%	$0.10	
Signature Preferred Card Not Present	2.40%	$0.10	Signature Preferred and Consumer Credit Spend cards that meet existing Services (3000-3999, 4112, 4411, 4511, 4722, 5812, 5814, 7011, 7512) r Social Service Organizations (8398) and Utilities (4900) not eligible for
Premium Consumer Credit Card Not Present	2.40%	$0.10	
Signature Pref Business to Business	2.10%	$0.10	Signature Preferred and Consumer Credit Spend cards that meet existing Visa. Eligible Merchants: Business-to-Business MCCs 0780, 1799, 2741 6300, 7311, 7333, 7349, 7361, 7372, 7375, 7379, 7392, 7399, 7829, 873-
Premium Consumer Credit Business to Business	2.10%	$0.10	
Signature Preferred Fuel	1.15%	$0.25	Signature Preferred and Consumer Credit Spend cards that meet existing that annual cardholder spend qualification threshold set by Visa. Eligible $1.10 per transaction. Maximum 2 days to deposit & settle.
Premium Consumer Credit Fuel	1.15%	$0.25	
Signature Preferred Standard	2.95%	$0.10	Signature Preferred and Consumer Credit Spend cards. Consumer Credit CPS qualified, Authorization required. Cap of $1.10 on transactions at Se
Premium Consumer Credit Standard	2.95%	$0.10	
Standard Credit and Signature Standard	2.70%	$0.10	Transaction date is more than three (3) days old. Authorization required. (4112), Cruise Lines (4411), Lodging (3501-3999, 7011), Car Rental (33 5967). Non-secure E-Commerce transactions. Maximum 30 days to depo
Standard Debit	1.90%	$0.25	
Standard Prepaid	1.90%	$0.25	
Commercial			
Business Card Present Debit	1.70%	$0.10	Business Debit cards and Business, Signature Business, Business Enhanc CPS/Supermarket, CPS/Restaurant, CPS/Service Station, CPS/Automate eligible for this program. Maximum 2 days to deposit & settle.
Commercial Retail Prepaid	2.15%	$0.10	
Business Card Not Present Debit	2.45%	$0.10	Business Debit cards and Business, Signature Business, Business Enhanc CPS/E-Commerce Basic, CPS/E-Commerce Preferred, CPS/Hotel & Car transactions at Utilities (4900) merchants can continue to qualify for the
Commercial Card Not Present Prepaid	2.65%	$0.10	

Gingergaye Hollowell
www.ElectronicMoneyCompany.com

RATE SCHEDULE (Effective April, 2014)

Transaction Qualification Information

pend, Signature Preferred Consumer cards and Business, Signature Business, and Business Enhanced cards that meet the existing CPS/Card Not Present, CPS/E-Commerce Basic, or CPS/E-Commerce Preferred. Consumer and Business debit and prepaid transactions it eligible for this program. Eligible Merchants: Utilities (4900). Requires registration with Visa and MVV must be present. Maximum 2

a pre-paid product, a brokerage account, or escrow account. Identified as E-Commerce transactions processed in a secure environment. address) required. E-Commerce requires additional data fields such as the merchant order number, valid E-Commerce indicator, and the and settlement. Authorization and settlement amounts must match. Purchase date must be within 1 day of auth date. Maximum 2 days to

tail Key-Entered requirements. Authorized. Mail or phone order and did not meet CPS/Card Not Present requirements. Did not meet 3299, 4112, 4511): last 13 positions of merchant name must contain either description of ancillary purchase or ticket number; ancillary ient number, issued in connection with ticket number, and passenger name). Authorization is Referral / Voice-Authorized transaction. ll payment indicators. Signature or Infinite card transactions, CPS qualified at Travel Services Merchants including, Airlines (3000-3299, 999, 7011), Car Rental (3351-3441, 7512), Travel Agencies (4722), Restaurants (5812), and Fast Food (5814). Cap of $0.95 on redit transactions at Service Stations (5541) and Automated Fuel Dispensers (5542). Maximum 3 days to deposit & settle.

or CPS/Card Not Present, CPS/E-Commerce Basic, or CPS/E-Commerce Preferred. Eligible Merchants: Tax Payments (9311). Requires within 1 day of auth date. Merchant can charge a convenience fee up to $3.95, which must be submitted as a separate transaction. Cap o deposit & settle.

PS/Card Not Present, CPS/E-Commerce Basic, or CPS/E-Commerce Preferred. Debt repayment indicator and Bill Payment indicators d Services (6012), Foreign Currency, Money Orders - Not Wire Transfer, Stored Value Card / Load, and Travelers Checks (6051). Cap on and MVV must be present. Maximum 2 days to deposit & settle.

requirements for EIRF. CPS-qualified, Signature Preferred and Consumer Credit Spend transactions at Travel Services merchants (3000- it Spend cards must meet that annual cardholder spend qualification threshold set by Visa. Maximum 2 days to deposit & settle.

requirements for CPS/Retail, CPS/Supermarket, CPS/Retail Key Entry, or CPS/Small Ticket at non Travel Services (3000-3999, 4112, Spend cards must meet that annual cardholder spend qualification threshold set by Visa. Charitable & Social Service Organizations s to deposit & settle.

requirements for CPS/Card Not Present, CPS/E-Commerce Basic, CPS/E-Commerce Preferred, CPS/Account Funding at non Travel merchants. Consumer Credit Spend cards must meet that annual cardholder spend qualification threshold set by Visa. Charitable & this program. Maximum 2 days to deposit & settle.

requirements for any CPS program. Consumer Credit Spend cards must meet that annual cardholder spend qualification threshold set by , 2791, 2842, 4214, 5021, 5039, 5044, 5046, 5047, 5051, 5065, 5074, 5085, 5099, 5131, 5137, 5139, 5169, 5192, 5193, 5198, 5199, 4, 8931, 8999. Maximum 2 days to deposit & settle.

requirements for CPS/Service Station, CPS/Automated Fuel Dispenser, and CPS/Small Ticket. Consumer Credit Spend cards must meet Merchants: Service Stations (5541) or Automated Fuel Dispensers (5542). Purchase date must be within 1 day of auth date. Cap of

Spend cards must meet that annual cardholder spend qualification threshold set by Visa. Transaction date is more than 2 days old. Not rvice Stations (5541) and Automated Fuel Dispensers (5542). Maximum 30 days to deposit & settle.

Signature or Infinite cards NOT CPS qualified at a Travel Services Merchant, including Airlines (3000-3299, 4511), Passenger Railway 51-3441, 7512), Travel Agencies (4722), Restaurants (5812), and Fast Food (5814). High-risk telemarketing transactions (5962, 5966, sit & settle.

ed, Corporate, and Purchasing Prepaid cards that meet existing requirements for CPS/Retail, CPS/Retail Key Entry, CPS/Small Ticket. d Fuel Dispenser, CPS/Hotel & Car Rental Card Present, or CPS/Passenger Transport Card Present. Quasi-Cash (6050, 6051) are

ed, Corporate, and Purchasing Prepaid cards that meet existing requirements for CPS/Card Not Present, Rental Card Not Present, CPS/Passenger Transport Card Not Present, or CPS/Account Funding. Business Debit and Prepaid Utilities program. Maximum 2 days to deposit & settle.

Secrets of Credit Card Processing Revealed
www.ElectronicMoneyCompany.com

INTERCHANGE

Program Rate Category	Rates Fee Per Sales $	Per Item	
Business Card Level 2	2.05%	$0.10	
Business Enhanced Level 2	2.05%	$0.10	Business, Signature Business, Business Enhanced, Corporate, Purchasing
Signature Business Level 2	2.05%	$0.10	5814, 7011, 7512). Level 2 data required, which is Sales Tax (sales tax m
Corporate Card Level 2	2.05%	$0.10	Purchasing card transactions at fuel merchants). Maximum 2 days to depo
Purchasing Card Level 2	2.05%	$0.10	
Purchasing Card Level 3	1.95%	$0.10	Purchasing, GSA Purchasing, and Corporate cards. CPS requirements mc includes Summary Record - Discount Amount, Freight / Shipping Amou Product Code, Quantity, Unit of Measure, Unit Cost, Discount per Line I
Corporate Card Level 3	1.95%	$0.10	Visa Payables Automation Service. Maximum 2 days to deposit & settle.
GSA Government to Government	1.65%	$0.10	GSA Purchasing Cards. Card Present / Magnetic Stripe Read / Signature government merchants only. Requires registration with Visa and MVV n
Business Electronic	2.40%	$0.10	
Business Enhanced Electronic	2.75%	$0.15	Business, Signature Business, Business Enhanced cards that meet existin Dispenser, CPS/Card Not Present, CPS/E-Commerce Preferred, CPS/E-C
Signature Business Electronic	2.85%	$0.20	7011, 7512). Corporate and Purchasing cards that meet Level 2 data requ
Corporate Electronic	2.75%	$0.10	Travel-Related Arrangement Services (5962), Direct Marketing - Outbo
Purchasing Electronic	2.75%	$0.10	transactions are not eligible for this program. Maximum 2 days to deposi
Business Retail	2.20%	$0.10	
Business Enhanced Retail	2.30%	$0.10	Business, Signature Business, Business Enhanced, Corporate, and Purch
Signature Business Retail	2.40%	$0.10	Station, or CPS/Auto Fuel Dispenser. Non-Travel Services transactions (
Corporate Retail	2.10%	$0.10	Maximum 2 days to deposit & settle.
Purchasing Retail	2.40%	$0.10	
Business Card Not Present	2.25%	$0.10	
Business Enhanced Card Not Present	2.45%	$0.15	Business, Signature Business, Business Enhanced, Corporate, and Purch
Signature Business Card Not Present	2.60%	$0.20	CPS/Account Funding. Non-Travel Services transactions (3000-3999, 4
Corporate Card Not Present	2.20%	$0.10	requirements (Sales Tax and Customer Code) are not met. Maximum 2 c
Purchasing Card Not Present	2.65%	$0.10	
Business Bus to Business	2.10%	$0.10	
Business Enhanced Bus to Business	2.25%	$0.10	Business, Signature Business, Enhanced Business, Corporate, and Purch
Signature Business Bus to Business	2.40%	$0.10	Business MCC's 0780, 1799, 2741, 2791, 2842, 4214, 5021, 5039, 5044,
Corporate Business to Business	2.10%	$0.10	7375, 7379, 7392, 7399, 7829, 8734, 8931, 8999. Level 2 data requirem
Purchasing Business to Business	2.40%	$0.10	
Corporate Card Travel Service	2.55%	$0.10	Corporate and Purchasing cards that meet existing requirements for any
Purchasing Card Travel Service	2.45%	$0.10	& settle.
Purchasing Electronic with Data	2.75%	$0.10	Non-GSA Purchasing and Corporate cards. Level 3 data requirements m Level 3 data requirements include Summary Record - Discount Amount Commodity Code, Item Descriptor, Product Code, Quantity, Unit of Me
Corporate Card Electronic with Data	2.75%	$0.10	Through Processing transactions via the Visa Payables Automation Serv
Business Standard	2.95%	$0.20	
Business Standard Debit	2.95%	$0.10	
Business Enhanced Standard	2.95%	$0.20	
Signature Business Standard	2.95%	$0.20	Business, Signature Business, Business Enhanced, Corporate, and Purch
Corporate Standard	2.95%	$0.10	
Purchasing Standard	2.95%	$0.10	
Commercial Standard Prepaid	2.95%	$0.10	
Large Ticket			
GSA Purchasing Card Large Ticket	1.20%	$39.00	GSA Purchasing cards that meet existing requirements for CPS/Retail, (and customer code) and Level 3 (Summary Record - Discount Amount, Code, Item Descriptor, Product Code, Quantity, Unit of Measure, Unit (3999, 4112, 4411, 4511, 4722, 5812, 5814, 7011, and 7512). Authoriza

Gingergaye Hollowell
www.ElectronicMoneyCompany.com

RATE SCHEDULE (Effective April, 2014)

Transaction Qualification Information

, and GSA Purchasing Cards. CPS requirements met. Non-Travel Services transactions (3000-3999, 4112, 4411, 4511, 4722, 5812, ust be between 0.1% and 22% of the sales amount - tax exempt transactions do not qualify) and Customer Code (only required for osit & settle.

t Non-Travel Services transactions (3000-3999, 4112, 4411, 4511, 4722, 5812, 5814, 7011, 7512). Level 3 data required, which nt, Duty Amount and Account Number and Line Item Detail Record - Item Sequence Number, Item Commodity Code, Item Descriptor, tem, Line Item Total, and Line Item Detail Indicator. Level 3 data is not required for Straight Through Processing transactions via the

Obtained / Authorized. CPS qualified. Eligible Merchants: Government Services (9399), Postal Services - Government (9402). Federal ust be present. Purchase date must be within 1 day of auth date. Maximum 2 days to deposit & settle.

g requirements for CPS/Retail, CPS/Supermarket, CPS/Retail Key Entry, CPS/Small Ticket, CPS/Service Station, CPS/Auto Fuel ommerce Basic, CPS/Retail 2, or CPS/Acct Funding for Travel Services transactions (3000-3999, 4112, 4411, 4511, 4722, 5812, 5814, irements (Sales Tax and Customer Code) but do not meet CPS requirements for Non-Travel Services transactions. Direct Marketing – und Telemarketing Merchants (5966), and Direct Marketing – Inbound Telemarketing Merchants (5967) and non-secure E-Commerce t & settle.

asing cards that meet existing requirements for CPS/Retail, CPS/Supermarket, CPS/Retail Key Entry, CPS/Small Ticket, CPS/Service 3000-3999, 4112, 4411, 4511, 4722, 5812, 5814, 7011, 7512). Level 2 data requirements (Sales Tax and Customer Code) are not met.

asing cards that meet existing requirements for CPS/Card Not Present, CPS/E-Commerce Basic, CPS/E-Commerce Preferred, or 112, 4411, 4511, 4722, 5812, 5814, 7011, 7512). Business, Signature Business, and Business Enhanced cards require AVS. Level 2 data lays to deposit & settle.

asing cards that meet existing requirements for any CPS program by non Travel Services merchants. Eligible Merchants: Business to 5046, 5047, 5051, 5065, 5074, 5085, 5099, 5131, 5137, 5139, 5169, 5192, 5193, 5198, 5199, 6300, 7311, 7333, 7349, 7361, 7372, ents (Sales Tax and Customer Code) are not met. Maximum 2 days to deposit & settle.

CPS program at Travel Services merchants (3000-3999, 4112, 4411, 4511, 4722, 5812, 5814, 7011, 7512). Maximum 2 days to deposit

et but CPS requirements not met for Non-Travel Services transactions (3000-3999, 4112, 4411, 4511, 4722, 5812, 5814, 7011, 7512). , Freight / Shipping Amount, Duty Amount and Account Number and Line Item Detail Record - Item Sequence Number, Item asure, Unit Cost, Discount per Line Item, Line Item Total, and Line Item Detail Indicator. Level 3 data is not required for Straight ice. Maximum 2 days to deposit & settle.

asing Cards. Transaction date is more than 2 days old. Not CPS qualified. Authorization required. Maximum 30 days to deposit & settle

CPS/Key Entry, CPS/Service Station, CPS/Card Not Present, CPS/E-Commerce Basic, or CPS/E-Commerce Preferred. Level 2 (sales tax , Freight / Shipping Amount, Duty Amount and Account Number and Line Item Detail Record - Item Sequence Number, Item Commodity Cost, Discount per Line Item, Line Item Total, and Line Item Detail Indicator) data is required. Not applicable to Travel Services (3000- tion required. Maximum 2 days to deposit & settle.

29

Visa® and MasterCard® Credit Vo...

This Credit Voucher Programs and Rate Schedule contains a summary of the primary qualification criteria established... conflict, the interchange requirements established by the Card Organizations (sometimes referred to associations) will...

Program Rate Category	Rates		
	Per Sales $	Per Item	
VISA*			
Consumer Credit			
US CRDT VCR-MOTO	2.05%	$0.00	Consumer Traditional Credit card transacti... and Passenger Railway (4112).
US CRDT VCR-Consumer	1.76%	$0.00	Consumer Traditional Credit card transacti... Commerce.
Debit			
US CRDT VCR-Debit	0.00%	$0.00	All Debit and Prepaid card transactions, in... and Card Organizations as being subject to...
Passenger Transport			
US CRDT VCR-Passenger Transport	2.33%	$0.00	Consumer Traditional Credit and Commerc...
Commercial Credit			
US CRDT VCR-Commercial Credit	2.35%	$0.00	Business, Signature Business, or Corporate...
US CRDT VCR-GSA Purchasing 1	2.35%	$0.00	GSA Purchasing card transactions ≤ $10,0...
US CRDT VCR-GSA Purchasing 2	2.15%	$0.00	GSA Purchasing card transactions > $10,0...
US CRDT VCR-GSA Purchasing 3	2.00%	$0.00	GSA Purchasing card transactions > $25,0...
US CRDT VCR-GSA Purchasing 4	1.80%	$0.00	GSA Purchasing card transactions > $100,0...
US CRDT VCR-GSA Purchasing 5	1.80%	$0.00	GSA Purchasing card transactions > $500,0...
US CRDT VCR-Purchasing 1	2.40%	$0.00	Purchasing card transactions ≤ $10,000. Al...
US CRDT VCR-Purchasing 2	2.30%	$0.00	Purchasing card transactions > $10,000 and...
US CRDT VCR-Purchasing 3	2.20%	$0.00	Purchasing card transactions > $25,000 and...
US CRDT VCR-Purchasing 4	2.00%	$0.00	Purchasing card transactions > $100,000 an...
US CRDT VCR-Purchasing 5	1.80%	$0.00	Purchasing card transactions > $500,000. A...

*Credit (or sales return) transactions for Account Funding and interregional transactions are applied back against the in...

Gingergaye Hollowell
www.ElectronicMoneyCompany.com

ucher Programs and Rate Schedule						(Effective April, 2014)

by Visa and MasterCard for most interchange programs - it is not all inclusive. In the event of any ambiguity or determine the interchange programs at which your transactions qualify.

Transaction Qualification Information

ons: Mail / Telephone Order and E-Commerce, except High Risk (5962, 5966, 5967), Airlines (3000-3299, 4511),

ons: All Industries, except Airlines (3000-3299, 4511), Passenger Railway (4112), Mail / Telephone Order, and E-

:luding Regulated Consumer Debit and Prepaid, Business Debit, and Commercial Prepaid Cards identified by Issuers the June 29, 2011 Federal Reserve final rule on Debit Card interchange.

:ial Credit card transactions: Airlines (3000-3299, 4511) and Passenger Railway (4112).

credit transactions. All Industries, except Airlines (3000-3299, 4511), and Passenger Railway (4112).
00. All Industries, except Airlines (3000-3299, 4511), and Passenger Railway (4112).
00 and ≤ $25,000. All Industries, except Airlines (3000-3299, 4511), and Passenger Railway (4112).
)0 and ≤ $100,000. All Industries, except Airlines (3000-3299, 4511), and Passenger Railway (4112).
)00 and ≤ $500,000. All Industries, except Airlines (3000-3299, 4511), and Passenger Railway (4112).
)00. All Industries, except Airlines (3000-3299, 4511), and Passenger Railway (4112).
l Industries, except Airlines (3000-3299, 4511), and Passenger Railway (4112).
l ≤ $25,000. All Industries, except Airlines (3000-3299, 4511), and Passenger Railway (4112).
l ≤ $100,000. All Industries, except Airlines (3000-3299, 4511), and Passenger Railway (4112).
id ≤ $500,000. All Industries, except Airlines (3000-3299, 4511), and Passenger Railway (4112).
.ll Industries, except Airlines (3000-3299, 4511), and Passenger Railway (4112).

:erchange program for which the purchase transaction originally qualified.

Secrets of Credit Card Processing Revealed
www.ElectronicMoneyCompany.com

INTERCHANGE F

This Interchange Rate Schedule contains a summary of the primary qualification criteria established by Visa®, Master inclusive. In the event of any ambiguity or conflict, the interchange requirements established by the Card Organization For a complete list, call the number on your merchant statement. Please note that Discover Network fees apply only to and fees, please call Customer Service.

Program Rate Category	Rates		
	Fee Per Sales $	Per Item	
MASTERCARD			
Merit III	1.58%	$0.10	Consumer, Enhanced, World, and World Elite cards. Face-to-Face / Mag
Merit III Enhanced	1.73%	$0.10	(3000-3299, 4511) and Passenger Railways (4112) transactions require g
World Merit III	1.77%	$0.10	Shops - 7230 for transactions up to $25). Authorization and settlement ar
High Value Merit III	2.20%	$0.10	(4112), and Limousines & Taxis (4121). Key-entered transactions, Servi
World Elite Merit III	2.20%	$0.10	3999, 7011), Cruise Lines (4411), Insurance (6300), and Real Estate Age
Merit III Debit	1.05%	$0.15	Railways (4112), Restaurants (5812), Travel Agencies (4722) are not eli
Regulated Debit	0.05%	$0.21	Regulated Consumer and Commercial Debit and Prepaid Cards identifie has NOT certified its fraud prevention procedures. Rate Indicator value i
Regulated Debit with Fraud Adjustment	0.05%	$0.22	Regulated Consumer and Commercial Debit and Prepaid Cards identifie has certified its fraud prevention procedures. Rate Indicator value identifi
Key Entered	1.89%	$0.10	
Key Entered Enhanced	2.04%	$0.10	Consumer, Enhanced, World, and World Elite cards at a non-T&E Merch
World Key Entered	2.05%	$0.10	eligible for this program. Authorization and settlement amounts can diffe
High Value Key Entered	2.50%	$0.10	(3000-3999, 4112, 4411, 4511, 7011, 7512, 7513, 7519). Automated Fue
World Elite Key Entered	2.50%	$0.10	Telecommunications (4812, 4814), Cable / Satellite (4899), Barber & Be
Key Entered Debit	1.60%	$0.15	days to deposit & settle.
Key Entered Prepaid	1.76%	$0.20	
Merit I	1.89%	$0.10	Consumer, Enhanced, World, and World Elite cards. Magnetic swipe not
Merit I Enhanced	2.04%	$0.10	order. Airlines (3000-3299, 4511) and Passenger Railways (4112) transa
World Merit I	2.05%	$0.10	Shops - 7230 for transactions up to $25). Authorization and settlement ar
High Value Merit I	2.50%	$0.10	(3351-3500, 7512, 7513, 7519), Cruise Line / Steamship (4411), Limous
World Elite Merit I	2.50%	$0.10	indicators present. Utilities (4900), Insurance (5960, 6300), and Real Est
Merit I Debit	1.60%	$0.15	3299, 4511), Passenger Railways (4112), Lodging (3501-3999, 7011), V Non face-to-face and E-Commerce transactions with all E-Commerce id
Merit I Prepaid	1.76%	$0.20	other merchants.
Small Ticket Debit	1.55%	$0.04	Consumer Debit cards. Transaction amount $15.00 or less / Magnetic str Taxis (4121), Bus Lines (4131), Bridge & Road Fees / Tolls (4784), Var Services - Family & Commercial (7211), Dry Cleaners (7216), Quick Co (7832), Videotape Rental Stores (7841), and Postal Services - Governme Restaurants (5812), Bars (5813), Fast Food (5814), and Limousines & T
Regulated Debit Small Ticket	0.05%	$0.21	Regulated Consumer and Commercial Debit and Prepaid Cards identifie
Regulated Debit Small Ticket with Fraud Adjustment	0.05%	$0.22	Indicator value identified by Issuers and Card Organizations of S (Regul Restaurants (5814) and Videotape Rental Stores (7841). Authorization a
Restaurant Debit	1.19%	$0.10	Consumer Debit cards. Magnetic Stripe read unless initiated via transpor Restaurants (5812). Transaction amount $60.00 or less for Restaurants (5
World Restaurant	1.73%	$0.10	
High Value Restaurant	2.20%	$0.10	World and World Elite cards. Magnetic Stripe read / Electronically Auth Restaurants (5812). Maximum 2 days to deposit & settle.
World Elite Restaurant	2.20%	$0.10	
Convenience Purchase	1.90%	$0.00	
Convenience Purchase Enhanced	1.90%	$0.00	Consumer, Enhanced, World, and World Elite cards. Magnetic Stripe rea
World Convenience Purchase	2.00%	$0.00	Theaters (7832), Limousines and Taxis (4121), and Variety Stores (5331 Authorization and settlement amounts do not have to match for Fast Foo
High Value Convenience Purchase	2.00%	$0.00	Maximum 2 days to deposit & settle.
World Elite Convenience Purchase	2.00%	$0.00	

Gingergaye Hollowell
www.ElectronicMoneyCompany.com

RATE SCHEDULE   (Effective April, 2014)

Card®, and Discover® Network (sometimes referred to as Discover) for most interchange programs - it is not all
s (sometimes referred to as associations) will determine the interchange programs at which your transactions qualify.
Discover transactions acquired by Bank of America Merchant Services. For more information regarding your Rates

---

Transaction Qualification Information

---

netic Stripe Read / Signature Obtained / Electronically Authorized. Eligible merchants include Retail and Restaurants (5812). Airline
eneral ticket information and trip leg data. Authorization and settlement amounts can differ up to 10% (up to 25% for Beauty and Barber
nounts do not have to match for Restaurants (5812), Bars (5813), Fast Food (5814), Airlines (3000-3299, 4511), Passenger Railways
ce Stations (5541), Automated Fuel Dispenser (5542), Utilities (4900), Vehicle Rental (3351-3500, 7512, 7513, 7519), Lodging (3501-
nts & Managers (6513) are not eligible for this program. World and World Elite transactions at Airlines (3000-3299, 4511), Passenger
gible for this program. Maximum 2 days to deposit & settle.

d by Issuers and Card Organizations as being subject to the June 29, 2011 Federal Reserve final rule on Debit Card interchange. Issuer
dentified by Issuers and Card Organizations of B (Base). Authorization required. Maximum 30 days to deposit & settle.

d by Issuers and Card Organizations as being subject to the June 29, 2011 Federal Reserve final rule on Debit Card interchange. Issuer
ied by Issuers and Card Organizations of I (Base plus Fraud Adjustment). Authorization required. Maximum 30 days to deposit & settle.

nant. Face-to-Face / Signature Obtained / Electronically Authorized. World & World Elite transactions at Restaurants (5812) are not
r up to 10%. Authorization and settlement amounts do not have to match for Restaurants (5812), Bars (5813), Fast Food (5814), T&E
l Dispenser (5542), Real Estate Agents & Managers (6513), Insurance (5960, 6300), Utilities (4900), Travel Agencies (4722).
auty Shops (7230), and Mail / Telephone Order (5962, 5964, 5965, 5966, 5967, 5968, 5969) not eligible for this program. Maximum 2

t required / Electronically Authorized / does not meet Key-Entered or Lodging & Auto Rental requirements. E-Commerce, Mail or Phone
ctions require general ticket information. Authorization and settlement amounts can differ up to 10% (up to 25% for Beauty & Barber
nounts do not have to match for Restaurants (5812), Bars (5813), Fast Food (5814), Lodging (3501-3999 or 7011), Vehicle Rental
ines & Taxis (4121), non face-to-face transactions (mail order and phone order), and E-Commerce transactions if all E-Commerce
ate Agents & Managers (6513) not eligible for this program. World and World Elite transactions at Restaurants (5812), Airlines (3000-
ehicle Rental (3351-3500, 7512, 7513, 7519), Cruise Lines / Steamships (4411), Travel Agencies (4722) not eligible for this program.
entifiers are exempt from timeliness edits. Maximum days to deposit & settle is 9 days for Airlines (3000-3299, 4511), 3 days for all

ipe read unless initiated via transponder / Electronically Authorized. Eligible Merchants: Commuter Transport (4111), Limousines &
iety Stores (5331), Convenience Stores (5499), Restaurants (5812), Fast Food (5814), News Dealers / Newsstands (5994), Laundry
py - Reproduction & Blueprinting Services (7338), Parking Lots and Garages (7523), Car Washes (7542), Motion Picture Theatres
nt (9402). Authorization and settlement amounts can differ up to 10%. Authorization and settlement amounts do not have to match for
axis (4121). Maximum 2 days to deposit & settle.

d by Issuers and Card Organizations as being subject to the June 29, 2011 Federal Reserve final rule on Debit Card interchange. Rate
ated Small Ticket Base). Transaction amount $10.00 or less / Card Present / Electronically Authorized. Eligible Merchants: Fast Food
nd settlement amounts do not have to match. Maximum 2 days to deposit & settle.

der / Electronically Authorized. Authorization and settlement amounts do not have to match. Eligible Merchants: Fast Food (5814) and
5812). Maximum 2 days to deposit & settle.

orized / Transactions amount $60.00 or less. Authorization and settlement amounts do not have to match. Eligible Merchants:

d unless initiated via transponder / Electronically Authorized. Eligible Merchants: Fast Food (5814), Convenience Stores (5499), Movie
). Transaction amount $25.00 or less for Limousines and Taxis (4121). Authorization and settlement amounts can differ up to 10%.
d (5814) and Limousines & Taxis (4121). Service Stations (5541) and Automated Fuel Dispenser (5542) not eligible for this program.

Secrets of Credit Card Processing Revealed
www.ElectronicMoneyCompany.com

INTERCHANGE F

Program Rate Category	Rates Fee Per Sales $	Per Item	
Emerging Markets Debit	0.80%	$0.25	Consumer Debit cards. Magnetic Swipe not required / Electronically Aut Fines (9222), Bail / Bond Payments (9223), Tax Payments (9311), Gover (8220), Schools and Educational Services not elsewhere classified (8299) (4784), Postal Services - Government (9402), and Passenger Railways (4 Passenger Railways (4112). Maximum 3 days to deposit & settle.
Merit I – Real Estate	1.10%	$0.00	
Merit I Enhanced - Real Estate	1.10%	$0.00	Consumer, Enhanced, World, and World Elite cards. Magnetic swipe not settlement amounts can differ up to 10%. Authorization and settlement a indicators present. Eligible Merchants: Real Estate Agents and Managers Maximum 3 days to deposit & settle.
World Merit I – Real Estate	1.10%	$0.00	
High Value Merit I – Real Estate	2.20%	$0.10	
World Elite Merit I – Real Estate	2.20%	$0.10	
Merit I – Real Estate Debit	1.10%	$0.00	
Merit I – Insurance	1.43%	$0.05	
Merit I Enhanced - Insurance	1.43%	$0.05	Consumer, Enhanced, World, and World Elite cards. Magnetic swipe not settlement amounts can differ up to 10%. Authorization and settlement a indicators present. Eligible Merchants: Direct Marketing Insurance Serv Commerce identifiers are exempt from timeliness edits. Maximum 3 day
World Merit I – Insurance	1.43%	$0.05	
High Value Merit I – Insurance	2.20%	$0.10	
World Elite Merit I – Insurance	2.20%	$0.10	
Merit I Consumer Loan	0.80%	$0.25	Consumer Debit cards. Magnetic swipe not required / Electronically Aut Quasi-Cash - Merchant (6051). Authorization and settlement amounts ca transactions if all E-Commerce indicators present. Requires registration a Commerce identifiers are exempt from timeliness edits. Maximum days t
Supermarket	1.48%	$0.10	
Supermarket Enhanced	1.48%	$0.10	
World Supermarket	1.58%	$0.10	Consumer, Enhanced, World, and World Elite cards. Face-to-Face / Mag consumer debit transactions only. Eligible Merchants: Supermarket (541
High Value Supermarket	1.90%	$0.10	
World Elite Supermarket	1.90%	$0.10	
Supermarket Debit	1.05%	$0.15	
Public Sector	1.55%	$0.10	
Public Sector Enhanced	1.55%	$0.10	Consumer, Enhanced, World and World Elite cards. Magnetic Swipe not Bond Payments (9223), Tax Payments (9311), Government Services (93 and Passenger Railways (4112). Authorization and settlement amounts c deposit & settle.
World Public Sector	1.55%	$0.10	
High Value Public Sector	1.55%	$0.10	
World Elite Public Sector	1.55%	$0.10	
Charities Credit	2.00%	$0.10	Consumer, Enhanced, World, World Elite, Business, Corporate, Purchas / Electronically Authorized. Eligible Merchant: Charitable & Social Serv with all E-Commerce identifiers are exempt from timeliness edits, and a
Charities Debit	1.45%	$0.15	
Standard	2.95%	$0.10	
Standard Enhanced	2.95%	$0.10	
World Standard	2.95%	$0.10	Consumer, Enhanced, World, and World Elite cards. Authorization requ
High Value Standard	3.25%	$0.10	
World Elite Standard	3.25%	$0.10	
Standard Debit	1.90%	$0.25	
Lodging & Auto Rental	1.58%	$0.10	Consumer and Enhanced cards. Magnetic swipe not required / Electronic Rental (Rental Agreement Number, Renter Name, Rental Return Addres Date, Folio Number, Property Phone Number, Customer Service Phone 7519), Lodging (3501-3999, 7011), and Cruise Lines (4411). Maximum
Lodging & Auto Rental Enhanced	1.80%	$0.10	
Lodging & Auto Rental Debit	1.15%	$0.15	
World T&E	2.30%	$0.10	World and World Elite cards. Magnetic Swipe not required / Electronica 7011), Travel Agencies (4722), Cruise Line / Steamship (4411) and Res amounts do not have to match. Airline, Vehicle Rental, and Lodging tran to deposit & settle.
High Value T&E	2.75%	$0.10	
World Elite T&E	2.75%	$0.10	

Gingergaye Hollowell
www.ElectronicMoneyCompany.com

RATE SCHEDULE (Effective April, 2014)

Transaction Qualification Information

horized. Eligible Merchants: Transportation (4111), Cable / Satellite / Other Pay Television / Radio Stations (4899), Court Costs (9211), nment Services (9399), Schools - Elementary & Secondary (8211), Colleges / Universities / Professional Schools / Junior Colleges , Direct Marketing Insurance Services (5960), Insurance Sales, Underwriting and Premiums (6300), Bridges & Road Fees / Tolls 112). Authorization and settlement amounts can differ up to 10%. Authorization and settlement amounts do not have to match for

required / Electronically Authorized / does not meet Key-Entered requirements. E-Commerce, Mail or Phone order. Authorization and nounts do not have to match for non face-to-face (mail order and phone order) and E-Commerce transactions if all E-Commerce Rentals (6513). Non face-to-face and E-Commerce transactions with all E-Commerce identifiers are exempt from timeliness edits.

required / Electronically Authorized / does not meet Key-Entered requirements. E-Commerce, Mail or Phone order. Authorization and nounts do not have to match for non face-to-face (mail order and phone order) and E-Commerce transactions if all E-Commerce ces (5960) and Insurance Sales, Underwriting, and Premiums (6300). Non face-to-face and E-Commerce transactions with all E-s to deposit & settle.

horized / does not meet Key-Entered or Lodging & Auto Rental requirements. E-Commerce, Mail or Phone order. Eligible Merchants: n differ up to 10% and do not have to match for non face-to-face transactions (mail order and phone order) and E-Commerce ind MasterCard Assigned ID (MAID) must be present. Cap of $2.95. Non face-to-face and E-Commerce transactions with all E-o deposit & settle is 3 days.

netic Stripe Read / Signature Obtained / Authorized. Authorization and settlement amounts can differ up to 10%. Cap of $0.35 on 1). Maximum 2 days to deposit & settle.

required / Electronically Authorized. Eligible Merchants: Court Costs & Alimony and Child Support (9211), Fines (9222), Bail and 99), Transportation - Suburban & Local Commuter (4111), Bridges & Road Fees / Tolls (4784), Postal Services - Government (9402), an differ up to 10%. Authorization and settlement amounts do not have to match for Passenger Railways (4112). Maximum 3 days to

ing, Fleet, Corporate World, Corporate World Elite, Business World, and Business World Elite cards. Magnetic Stripe read not required ice Organizations (8398). Authorization and settlement amounts can differ up to 10%. Non face-to-face and E-Commerce transactions ithorization and settlement amounts do not have to match. Maximum 3 days to deposit & settle.

ired. Maximum 30 days to deposit & settle.

ally Authorized. Requires enriched data fields in authorization and settlement. Transactions must include mandatory fields of Vehicle s, Rental Return Date, Rental Check-out Date, Customer Service Phone Number) or Lodging Addendum record (Arrival Date, Departure Number). Authorization and settlement amounts do not have to match. Eligible Merchants: Vehicle Rental (3351-3500, 7512, 7513, 2 days to deposit & settle.

lly Authorized. Eligible Merchants: Airlines (3000-3299, 4511), Vehicle Rental (3351-3500, 7512, 7513, 7519), Lodging (3501-3999 or aurants (5812). World Elite transactions at Airlines (3000-3299, 4511) are not eligible for this program. Authorization and settlement sactions must be accompanied by a Passenger Transport, Vehicle Rental, or Lodging addendum record, respectively. Maximum 3 days

Secrets of Credit Card Processing Revealed
www.ElectronicMoneyCompany.com

INTERCHANGE

Program Rate Category	Rates Fee Per Sales $	Per Item	
High Value T&E Large Ticket	2.00%	$0.00	High Value World and World Elite cards. Eligible Merchants: Airlines (
World Elite T&E Large Ticket	2.00%	$0.00	Steamship (4411), Travel Agencies (4722), and Restaurants (5812). Mag $2,500 or greater. Airline, Vehicle Rental, and Lodging transactions mus and settle.
Petroleum CAT / AFD Debit	0.70%	$0.17	Consumer Debit cards. Transaction at Cardholder Activated Terminal or advice with the total amount spent by the cardholder is submitted within Merchants: Automated Fuel Dispenser (5542). Cap of $0.95. Maximum
Petroleum Service Station Debit	0.70%	$0.17	Consumer Debit cards. Magnetic Stripe read unless initiated via transpo
Petroleum	1.90%	$0.00	
Petroleum Enhanced	1.90%	$0.00	Consumer, Enhanced, World, and World Elite cards. Eligible Merchants
World Petroleum	2.00%	$0.00	transponder or completion authorization advice with the total amount sp
High Value Petroleum	2.00%	$0.00	Maximum 2 days to deposit & settle.
World Elite Petroleum	2.00%	$0.00	
Passenger Transport	1.75%	$0.10	
Passenger Transport Enhanced	1.90%	$0.10	Consumer and Enhanced cards. Eligible Merchants: Airlines (3000-3299 Additional addendum data required, including Passenger Name, Ticket I
Passenger Transport Debit	1.60%	$0.15	
High Value Airline	2.30%	$0.10	High Value World and World Elite cards. Eligible Merchants: Airlines (Name, Ticket Number, and Issuing Carrier), Trip Leg data (Travel date,
World Elite Airline	2.30%	$0.10	amounts do not have to match. Maximum 3 days to deposit & settle.
Full UCAF	1.68%	$0.10	
Full UCAF Enhanced	1.83%	$0.10	Consumer, Enhanced, World, and World Elite cards and Online Checko
World Full UCAF	1.87%	$0.10	type must indicate Electronic Commerce Transactions and merchant and Protocol and Cardholder Authentication in authorization. T&E merchan
High Value Full UCAF	2.30%	$0.10	(4900), and Automated Fuel Dispensers (5542) not eligible for this prog
World Elite Full UCAF	2.30%	$0.10	Railways (4112), Restaurants (5812), and Travel Agencies (4722) not el
Full UCAF Debit	1.15%	$0.15	deposit & settle.
Merchant UCAF	1.58%	$0.10	Consumer, Enhanced, World, and World Elite cards and Online Checko
Merchant UCAF Enhanced	1.73%	$0.10	must indicate Electronic Commerce Transactions and merchant's partici
World Merchant UCAF	1.77%	$0.10	Cardholder Authentication in authorization. T&E merchants require add
High Value Merchant UCAF	2.20%	$0.10	Automated Fuel Dispensers (5542) not eligible for this program. Debit t
World Elite Merchant UCAF	2.20%	$0.10	(3000-3299, 4511), Passenger Railways (4112), Restaurants (5812), and
Merchant UCAF Debit	1.05%	$0.15	timeliness edits. Maximum 2 days to deposit & settle.
Service Industries	1.15%	$0.05	
Service Industries Enhanced	1.15%	$0.05	
World Service Industries	1.15%	$0.05	Consumer, Enhanced, World, and World Elite cards. Requires a recurri swipe not required / Electronically Authorized. Authorization and settle
High Value Service Industries	1.15%	$0.05	deposit & settle.
World Elite Service Industries	1.15%	$0.05	
Services Industries Debit	1.15%	$0.05	
Utilities	0.00%	$0.65	
Utilities Enhanced	0.00%	$0.65	
Utilities World	0.00%	$0.65	
Utilities High Value	0.00%	$0.75	
Utilities World Elite	0.00%	$0.75	Consumer, Enhanced, World, World Elite, Business, Business World, a
Utilities Debit	0.00%	$0.45	settlement amounts can differ up to 10%. Eligible merchant: Utilities (4
Utilities Prepaid	0.00%	$0.65	cardholder spend (reviewed quarterly by MasterCard): Business - spend
Utilities Business	0.00%	$1.50	≥ $50,000 and < $100,000; Business Level 4 - spend ≥ $100,000. For c
Utilities Business Debit	0.00%	$1.50	program, and Business World Elite transactions will qualify for the Bus
Utilities Business Level 2/World	0.00%	$1.50	Maximum 2 days to deposit & settle.
Utilities Bus Level 3/World Elite	0.00%	$1.50	
Utilities Business Level 4	0.00%	$1.50	
Utilities Business World	0.00%	$1.50	
Utilities Business World Elite	0.00%	$1.50	

Gingergaye Hollowell
www.ElectronicMoneyCompany.com

RATE SCHEDULE (Effective April, 2014)

Transaction Qualification Information

3000-3299 or 4511), Automobile / Vehicle Rental (3351-3500, 7512, 7513, 7519), Lodging (3501-3999 or 7011), Cruise Line / netic Swipe not required / Electronically Authorized. Authorization and settlement amounts do not have to match. Transaction amount t be accompanied by a Passenger Transport, Vehicle Rental, or Lodging addendum record, respectively. Maximum of 3 days to deposit

Automated Fuel Dispenser. Electronically Authorized. Magnetic Stripe read unless initiated via transponder or completion authorization 60 minutes of the authorization for Automated Fuel Dispenser (5542) merchants. CAT level indicator of 1 or 2 must be present. Eligible 2 days to deposit & settle.

der / Electronically Authorized. Eligible Merchants: Service Station (5541). Cap of $0.95. Maximum 2 days to deposit & settle.

: Service Stations (5541) and Automated Fuel Dispenser (5542). Electronically Authorize. Magnetic Stripe read unless initiated via ent by the cardholder is submitted within 60 minutes of the authorization for Automated Fuel Dispenser (5542) merchants. Cap of $0.95.

), 4511). Magnetic Swipe read not required / Electronically Authorized. Authorization and settlement amounts do not have to match. Number, Issuing Carrier and Itinerary Data in Settlement. Maximum 9 days to deposit & settle.

3000-3299, 4511). Magnetic swipe read not required / Authorized. Airlines / Passenger transport detail - General Ticket data (Passenger Carrier Code, Service Class Code, City of origin / Airport code, City of destination / Airport code). Authorization and settlement

ut Service transactions. Magnetic swipe not required / Electronically Authorized. Merchant must support SecureCode software. Terminal I issuer's participation in MasterCard UCAF. UCAF indicator of 2 must be present. Must have valid Security level indicator / Security ts require addendum data. Vehicle Rental (3351-3500, 7512, 7513, 7519), Lodging (3501-3999, 7011), Cruise Lines (4411), Utilities ram. Debit transactions at Insurance (5960, 6300) and World and World Elite transactions at Airlines (3000-3299, 4511), Passenger igible for this program. E-Commerce transactions with all E-Commerce indicators are exempt from timeliness edits. Maximum 2 days to

ut Service transactions. Magnetic swipe not required / Electronically Authorized. Merchant must use SecureCode software. Terminal type pation in MasterCard UCAF. UCAF indicator of 1 must be present. Must have valid Security level indicator / Security protocol and endum data. Vehicle Rental (3351-3500, 7512, 7513, 7519), Lodging (3501-3999, 7011), Cruise Lines (4411), Utilities (4900), and ransactions at Insurance (5960, 6300) and Real Estate Agents & Managers (6513) and World and World Elite transactions at Airlines l Travel Agencies (4722) not eligible for this program. E-Commerce transactions with all E-Commerce indicators are exempt from

ng payment transaction. Cardholder must not be present and authorization request must have value of 4 in Point of Sale data. Magnetic ment amounts can differ up to 10%. Eligible Merchants: Phone Service (4814) and Cable TV / Satellite (4899). Maximum 2 days to

nd Business World Elite cards. Registration not required. Magnetic swipe not required / Electronically Authorized. Authorization and 900). Transactions on Business cards that participate in Small Business Spend Processing will qualify for programs based on annual 1 - $25,000; Business Level 2 (formally known as Business Enhanced Value) - spend> $25,000 and - $50,000; Business Level 3 - spend ards that do not participate in Small Business Spend Processing, Business World transactions will qualify for the Business Level 2 iness Level 3 program. Cable, Satellite, TV and Radio (4899) and Telecommunications (4812) merchants are not eligible for this program

Secrets of Credit Card Processing Revealed
www.ElectronicMoneyCompany.com

INTERCHANGE I

Program Rate Category	Rates		
	Fee Per Sales $	Per Item	
Payment Transaction	0.19%	$0.53	Consumer cards. Magnetic Stripe Read not required / Electronically Auth Institution (6532) and Payment Service Provider - Merchant (6533).
Payment Transaction Debit	0.19%	$0.53	
Lrg Mkt Corp Payment Transaction	0.19%	$0.53	
Lrg Mkt Corp World Payment Trans	0.19%	$0.53	
LrgMkt Corp Wrld Elite Pymnt Tran	0.19%	$0.53	Business, Corporate, Purchasing, Corporate World, Corporate World Elit amounts do not match. Eligible Merchants: Payment Service Provider - M
Business Payment Transaction	0.19%	$0.53	
Bus World Payment Transaction	0.19%	$0.53	
Bus Wrld Elite Payment Transaction	0.19%	$0.53	
Electronic Payment Account	0.19%	$0.53	Electronic Payment Account. Magnetic swipe not required / Authorizatio Amount, and Customer Code (when provided by customer). Eligible Mer Supermarkets (5411), Telephone (4813, 4814), and Warehouse Club (530
Comml Payments Acct Lrg Tckt 1	1.20%	$0.00	Commercial Payments Account cards. Magnetic Stripe read not required summary addendum data. Transactions will qualify based on transaction and ≤ $1,000,000; Tier 5 - > $1,000,000. Authorization and settlement ar (3501-3999, 7011), Cruise Lines (4411), Automated Fuel Dispensers (55 (4112), and Restaurants (5812) not eligible for this program. Non face-to settle.
Comml Payments Acct Lrg Tckt 2	1.00%	$0.00	
Comml Payments Acct Lrg Tckt 3	0.90%	$0.00	
Comml Payments Acct Lrg Tckt 4	0.80%	$0.00	
Comml Payments Acct Lrg Tckt 5	0.70%	$0.00	
Large Market Corp Large Ticket I	1.25%	$40.00	
Large Market Corp World Lrg Tkt I	1.25%	$40.00	
Lrg Mkt Corp World Elite Lrg Tkt I	1.25%	$40.00	Business, Corporate, Purchasing, Fleet, Corporate World, Corporate Wor Electronically Authorized. Transaction amount greater than $7,255 and k Code, Item Description, Item Quantity, Item Unit of Measure, Extended transaction information addendum. ID Number, Driver Number, and Veh Authorization and settlement amounts can differ up to 25%. Authorizatio (5814), Lodging (3501-3999 or 7011), and E-Commerce transactions wit programs based on annual cardholder spend (reviewed quarterly by Mast Business Level 3 - spend ≥ $50,000 and < $100,000; Business Level 4 - s Business Level 2 program, and Business World Elite transactions will qu (4112), and Restaurants (5812) merchants not eligible for this program. E this program. Non face-to-face and E-Commerce transactions with all E-
Business Large Ticket I	1.20%	$40.00	
Business Large Ticket I Lodging	2.30%	$0.10	
Business Debit Large Ticket I	1.25%	$40.00	
Bus Debit Large Ticket I Lodging	2.30%	$0.10	
Lrg Mkt Purchasing Large Ticket I	1.25%	$40.00	
Large Market Fleet Large Ticket I	1.25%	$40.00	
Bus Level 2/World Large Ticket I	1.36%	$40.00	
Bus Level 3/World Elite Large Tkt I	1.41%	$40.00	
Business Level 4 Large Ticket I	1.51%	$40.00	
Business World Large Ticket I	1.36%	$40.00	
Business World Elite Large Ticket I	1.41%	$40.00	
Large Market Corp Large Ticket II	1.20%	$60.00	
Large Market Corp World Lrg Tkt II	1.20%	$60.00	
Lrg Mkt Corp World Elite Lrg Tkt II	1.20%	$60.00	
Business Large Ticket II	1.20%	$40.00	Business, Corporate, Purchasing, Fleet, Corporate World, Corporate Wor Electronically Authorized. Transaction amount greater than $25,000 and Code, Item Description, Item Quantity, Item Unit of Measure, Extended transaction information addendum. ID Number, Driver Number, and Veh Authorization and settlement amounts can differ up to 25%. Authorizatio (5814), Lodging (3501-3999 or 7011), and E-Commerce transactions wit programs based on annual cardholder spend (reviewed quarterly by Mast Business Level 3 - spend ≥ $50,000 and < $100,000; Business Level 4 - s Business Level 2 program, and Business World Elite transactions will qu (4112), and Restaurants (5812) merchants not eligible for this program. E this program. Non face-to-face and E-Commerce transactions with all E-
Business Large Ticket II Lodging	2.30%	$0.10	
Business Debit Large Ticket II	1.25%	$40.00	
Bus Debit Large Ticket II Lodging	2.30%	$0.10	
Lrg Mkt Purchasing Large Ticket II	1.20%	$60.00	
Large Market Fleet Large Ticket II	1.20%	$60.00	
Bus Level 2/World Large Ticket II	1.36%	$40.00	
Bus Level 3/World Elite Large Tkt II	1.41%	$40.00	
Business Level 4 Large Ticket II	1.51%	$40.00	
Business World Large Ticket II	1.36%	$40.00	
Business World Elite Large Ticket II	1.41%	$40.00	

Gingergaye Hollowell
www.ElectronicMoneyCompany.com

RATE SCHEDULE (Effective April, 2014)

Transaction Qualification Information

...orized. Authorization and settlement amounts do not match. Eligible Merchants: Payment Service Provider - Member Financial

...e, Business World, Business World Elite cards. Magnetic Stripe Read / Electronically Authorized. Authorization and settlement ...Member Financial Institution (6532) and Payment Service Provider - Merchant (6533). Maximum 3 days to deposit and settle.

...n required. Authorization and settlement amounts do not have to match. Must include the actual Payment Reference Number, Tax ...chants: Cruise Lines (4411), Bars (5813), Fast Food (5814), Mail / Telephone Order (5960, 5962, 5964, 5965, 5966, 5967, 5968, 5969), ...0). Maximum 3 days to deposit & settle.

/ Electronically Authorized. Provide Tax Amount and Customer Code (when provided by customer). Lodging requires Lodging amount; Tier 1 - ~ $7,255 and≤ $25,000; Tier 2 - ~ $25,000 and ≤ $100,000; Tier 3 - ~ $100,000 and ≤ $500,000; Tier 4 - ~ $500,000 ...nounts can differ up to 10%. Authorization and settlement amounts do not have to match for Bars (5813), Fast Food (5814), Lodging ...42), and Limousines & Taxis (4121). Airlines (3000-3299, 4511), Vehicle Rental (3351-3500, 7512, 7513, 7519), Passenger Railways -face and E-Commerce transactions with all E-Commerce identifiers are exempt from timeliness edits. Maximum 2 days to deposit &

...ld Elite, Business World, Business World Elite cards. Magnetic Swipe read required only for Fleet card transactions at fuel locations / ...ess than $25,000. Provide Tax Amount, Customer Code (when provided by customer), Corporate line item transaction detail (Product Item Amount, Debit or Credit Indicator). Fleet card transactions (at fuel locations) for fuel and non-fuel purchases must provide ...icle Number must match in authorization and clearing for Fleet card transactions. Lodging requires Lodging summary addendum data. ...n and settlement amounts do not have to match for Cruise Lines (4411), Automated Fuel Dispensers (5542), Bars (5813), Fast Food ...h all E-Commerce indicators. Transactions on Business cards that participate in Small Business Spend Processing will qualify for ...erCard): Business - spend ~ $25,000; Business Level 2 (formally known as Business Enhanced Value) - spend ~ $25,000 and ~ $50,000; ...spend ≥ $100,000. For cards that do not participate in Small Business Spend Processing, Business World transactions will qualify for the ...alify for the Business Level 3 program. Airlines (3000-3299, 4511), Vehicle Rental (3351-3500, 7512, 7513, 7519), Passenger Railways ...Business Level 2 through 4, Corporate, Purchasing, and Fleet card transactions at Lodging (3501-3999, 7011) merchants not eligible for Commerce indicators are exempt from timeliness edits. Maximum 2 days to deposit & settle.

...ld Elite, Business World, Business World Elite cards. Magnetic Swipe read required only for Fleet card transactions at fuel locations / ...less than $100,000. Provide Tax Amount, Customer Code (when provided by customer), Corporate line item transaction detail (Product Item Amount, Debit or Credit Indicator). Fleet card transactions (at fuel locations) for fuel and non-fuel purchases must provide ...icle Number must match in authorization and clearing for Fleet card transactions. Lodging requires Lodging summary addendum data. ...n and settlement amounts do not have to match for Cruise Lines (4411), Automated Fuel Dispensers (5542), Bars (5813), Fast Food ...h all E-Commerce indicators. Transactions on Business cards that participate in Small Business Spend Processing will qualify for ...erCard): Business - spend ~ $25,000; Business Level 2 (formally known as Business Enhanced Value) - spend ~ $25,000 and ~ $50,000; ...spend ≥ $100,000. For cards that do not participate in Small Business Spend Processing, Business World transactions will qualify for the ...alify for the Business Level 3 program. Airlines (3000-3299, 4511), Vehicle Rental (3351-3500, 7512, 7513, 7519), Passenger Railways ...Business Level 2 through 4, Corporate, Purchasing, and Fleet card transactions at Lodging (3501-3999, 7011) merchants not eligible for Commerce indicators are exempt from timeliness edits. Maximum 2 days to deposit & settle.

Secrets of Credit Card Processing Revealed
www.ElectronicMoneyCompany.com

INTERCHANGE

Program Rate Category	Rates	
	Fee Per Sales $	Per Item
Large Market Corp Large Ticket III	1.15%	$80.00
Lrg Mkt Corp World Lrg Tkt III	1.15%	$80.00
Lrg Mkt Corp Wrld Elite Lrg Tkt III	1.15%	$80.00
Business Large Ticket III	1.20%	$40.00
Business Large Ticket III Lodging	2.30%	$0.10
Business Debit Large Ticket III	1.25%	$40.00
Bus Debit Large Ticket III Lodging	2.30%	$0.10
Lrg Mkt Purchasing Large Ticket III	1.15%	$80.00
Large Market Fleet Large Ticket III	1.15%	$80.00
Bus Level 2/World Large Ticket III	1.36%	$40.00
Bus Level 3/World Elite Lrg Tkt III	1.41%	$40.00
Business Level 4 Large Ticket III	1.51%	$40.00
Business World Large Ticket III	1.36%	$40.00
Bus World Elite Large Ticket III	1.41%	$40.00
Large Market Corp Face to Face	2.50%	$0.10
Lrg Mkt Corp World Face to Face	2.50%	$0.10
Large Market Corp World Elite F2F	2.50%	$0.10
Business Face to Face	2.00%	$0.10
Business Debit Face to Face	2.20%	$0.10
Large Market Purchasing F2F	2.50%	$0.10
Large Market Fleet Face to Face	2.50%	$0.10
Bus Level 2/World Face to Face	2.16%	$0.10
Business Level 3/World Elite F2F	2.21%	$0.10
Business Level 4 Face to Face	2.31%	$0.10
Business World Face to Face	2.16%	$0.10
Business World Elite Face to Face	2.21%	$0.10
Lrg Mkt Corp Face to Face Petro	2.05%	$0.10
Lrg Mkt Corp World F2F Petroleum	2.05%	$0.10
Lrg Mkt Corp World Elite F2F Petro	2.05%	$0.10
Business Face to Face Petroleum	2.00%	$0.10
Bus Debit Face to Face Petroleum	2.05%	$0.10
Large Market Purchasing F2F Petro	2.05%	$0.10
Bus Level 2/World F2F Petroleum	2.16%	$0.10
Bus Level 3/World Elite F2F Petro	2.21%	$0.10
Business Level 4 F2F Petroleum	2.31%	$0.10
Large Market Corp Data Rate I	2.65%	$0.10
Lrg Mkt Corp World Data Rate I	2.65%	$0.10
Large Market Corp World Elite DR I	2.65%	$0.10
Business Data Rate I	2.65%	$0.10
Business Debit Data Rate I	2.65%	$0.10
Business Level 2/World Data Rate I	2.81%	$0.10
Bus Level 3/World Elite Data Rate I	2.86%	$0.10
Business Level 4 Data Rate I	2.96%	$0.10
Business World Data Rate I	2.81%	$0.10
Business World Elite Data Rate I	2.86%	$0.10

Business, Corporate, Purchasing, Fleet, Corporate World, Corporate Wor Electronically Authorized. Transaction amount greater than $100,000. Pr Description, Item Quantity, Item Unit of Measure, Extended Item Amou information addendum. ID Number, Driver Number, and Vehicle Numbe Authorization and settlement amounts can differ up to 25%. Authorizatio (5814), Lodging (3501-3999 or 7011), and E-Commerce transactions wit programs based on annual cardholder spend (reviewed quarterly by Mast Business Level 3 - spend ≥ $50,000 and ~$100,000; Business Level 4 - Business Level 2 program, and Business World Elite transactions will qu (4112), and Restaurants (5812) merchants not eligible for this program. F this program. Non face-to-face and E-Commerce transactions with all E-

Business, Corporate, Purchasing, Fleet, Corporate World, Corporate Wor Authorized. Transactions at non-fuel locations must provide Tax Amoun Transportation - Suburban & Local Commuter Passenger (4111), Bus Li (5499), Fuel Dealers (5983), Schools (8211), Colleges / Universities / Pr (9211), Fines (9222), Tax Payments (9311), Government Services (9399 to 25% for Barber & Beauty Shops - 7230). Authorization and settlemen on Business cards that participate in Small Business Spend Processing w Level 2 (formally known as Business Enhanced Value) - spend ≥ $25,000 participate in Small Business Spend Processing, Business World transact Airlines (3000-3299, 4511), Vehicle Rental (3351-3500, 7513, 751 Order (5960, 5962, 5964-5969) merchants are not eligible for this progra with all E-Commerce indicators are exempt from timeliness edits. Maxin

Corporate, Corporate World, Corporate World Elite, Business, Business Authorized. Transactions at non-fuel locations must provide Tax Amoun Dispenser (5542), Convenience Stores (5499), Fuel Dealers (5983), U.K for Automated Fuel Dispensers (5542). Non face-to-face and E-Commer

Business, Corporate, Purchasing, Fleet, Corporate World, Corporate Wo Authorized. Authorization and settlement amounts do not have to match Business cards that participate in Small Business Spend Processing will 2 (formally known as Business Enhanced Value) - spend ≥ $25,000 and in Small Business Spend Processing, Business World transactions will q (3000-3299, 4511), Vehicle Rental (3351-3500, 7512, 7513, 7519), Lod days to deposit & settle.

Gingergaye Hollowell
www.ElectronicMoneyCompany.com

RATE SCHEDULE (Effective April, 2014)

Transaction Qualification Information

ld Elite, Business World, Business World Elite cards. Magnetic Swipe read required only for Fleet card transactions at fuel locations. ovide Tax Amount, Customer Code (when provided by customer), Corporate line item transaction detail (Product Code, Item at, Debit or Credit Indicator). Fleet card transactions (at fuel locations) for fuel and non-fuel purchases must provide transaction r must match in authorization and clearing for Fleet card transactions. Lodging requires Lodging summary addendum data. n and settlement amounts do not have to match for Cruise Lines (4411), Automated Fuel Dispensers (5542), Bars (5813), Fast Food h all E-Commerce indicators. Transactions on Business cards that participate in Small Business Spend Processing will qualify for erCard): Business - spend ~ $25,000; Business Level 2 (formally known as Business Enhanced Value) - spend ≥ $25,000 and ~ $50,000; spend ≥ $100,000. For cards that do not participate in Small Business Spend Processing, Business World transactions will qualify for the alify for the Business Level 3 program. Airlines (3000-3299, 4511), Vehicle Rental (3351-3500, 7512, 7513, 7519), Passenger Railways usiness Level 2 through 4, Corporate, Purchasing, and Fleet card transactions at Lodging (3501-3999, 7011) merchants not eligible for Commerce indicators are exempt from timeliness edits. Maximum 2 days to deposit & settle.

ld Elite, Business World, Business World Elite cards. Face to Face Magnetic Stripe Read / Signature Obtained / Electronically t & Customer Code (when provided by customer). Tax Amount must be between 0.1% to 30% of the sales amount, except for nes (4131), Courier Services (4215), Marinas (4468), Bridge & Road Fees / Tolls (4784), Service Stations (5541), Convenience Stores ofessional Schools (8220), Charitable Organizations (8398), Religious Organizations (8661), Court Costs / Alimony / Child Support), Postal Services - Government (9402), and UK Petrol Stations (9752). Authorization and settlement amounts can differ up to 10% (up t amounts do not have to match for Cruise Lines (4411), Limousines & Taxis (4121), Bars (5813), and Fast Food (5814). Transactions ill qualify for programs based on annual cardholder spend (reviewed quarterly by MasterCard): Business - spend ~ $25,000; Business) and ~ $50,000; Business Level 3 - spend ≥ $50,000 and ~ $100,000; Business Level 4 - spend ≥ $100,000. For cards that do not ions will qualify for the Business Level 2 program, and Business World Elite transactions will qualify for the Business Level 3 program, 19), Lodging (3501-3999, 7011), Passenger Railways (4112), Automated Fuel Dispenser (5542), Restaurants (5812), and Mail / Phone m. MasterCard Corporate Fleet card at fuel locations are not eligible for this program. Non face-to-face and E-Commerce transactions num 2 days to deposit & settle.

World, Business World Elite, Purchasing, and Fleet cards. Face to Face / Magnetic Stripe Read / Signature Obtained / Electronically t & Customer Code (when provided by customer). Eligible Merchants: Marinas (4468), Service Stations (5541), Automated Fuel . Petro (9752). Authorization and settlement amounts can differ up to 10%. Authorization and settlement amounts do not have to match ce transactions with all E-Commerce indicators are exempt from timeliness edits. Maximum 2 days to deposit & settle.

rld Elite, Business World, Business World Elite, and Electronic Payment Account cards. Magnetic Swipe not required / Electronically Corporate Fleet card (at fuel locations) for fuel and non-fuel purchases provide transaction information addendum. Transactions on qualify for programs based on annual cardholder spend (reviewed quarterly by MasterCard): Business - spend ~ $25,000; Business Level ~ $50,000; Business Level 3 - spend ≥ $50,000 and ~ $100,000; Business Level 4 - spend ≥ $100,000. For cards that do not participate ualify for the Business Level 2 program, and Business World Elite transactions will qualify for the Business Level 3 program. Airlines ging (3501-3999, 7011), Passenger Railways (4112), and Restaurants (5812) merchants are not eligible for this program. Maximum 3

Secrets of Credit Card Processing Revealed
www.ElectronicMoneyCompany.com

INTERCHANGE R

Program Rate Category	Rates Fee Per Sales $	Per Item	
Large Market Corp Data Rate II	2.50%	$0.10	
Lrg Mkt Corp World Data Rate II	2.50%	$0.10	
Lrg Mkt Corp World Elite DR II	2.50%	$0.10	Business, Corporate, Purchasing, Fleet, Corporate World, Corporate World transactions at fuel locations / Electronically Authorized. Authorization an Corporate card transactions and for Purchasing and Fleet card transactions Commuter Passenger (4111), Bus Lines (4131), Courier Services (4215), (5499), Fuel Dealers (5983), Schools (8211), Colleges / Universities / Prof (9211), Fines (9222), Tax Payments (9311), Government Services (9399), purchases provide transaction information addendum. Transactions on Bu quarterly by MasterCard): Business - spend ~ $25,000; Business Level 2 (Business Level 4 - spend ≥ $100,000. For cards that do not participate in S transactions will qualify for the Business Level 3 program. Airlines (3000 (5812) merchants are not eligible for this program. Non face-to-face trans
Business Data Rate II	2.00%	$0.10	
Business Debit Data Rate II	2.20%	$0.10	
Lrg Mkt Purchasing Data Rate II	2.50%	$0.10	
Large Market Fleet Data Rate II	2.50%	$0.10	
Business Level 2/World Data Rate II	2.16%	$0.10	
Bus Level 3/World Elite Data Rate II	2.21%	$0.10	
Business Level 4 Data Rate II	2.31%	$0.10	
Business World Data Rate II	2.16%	$0.10	
Business World Elite Data Rate II	2.21%	$0.10	
Lrg Mkt Corp Data Rate II Petro	2.05%	$0.10	
Lrg Mkt Corp World DR II Petro	2.05%	$0.10	
Lge Mkt Corp Wrld Elite DRII Petro	2.05%	$0.10	
Business Data Rate II Petroleum	2.00%	$0.10	Corporate, Corporate World, Corporate World Elite, Business, Business V Electronically Authorized. Authorization and settlement amounts do not h and for Purchasing and Fleet card transactions at non-fuel locations. Elgi (5983), U.K. Petro (9752). Non face-to-face transactions are exempt from
Bus Debit Data Rate II Petroleum	2.05%	$0.10	
Lrg Mkt Purchasing DR II Petro	2.05%	$0.10	
Lrg Mkt Fleet Data Rate II Petro	2.05%	$0.10	
Bus Level 2/World DR II Petroleum	2.16%	$0.10	
Bus Level 3/World Elite DR II Petro	2.21%	$0.10	
Business Level 4 DR II Petroleum	2.31%	$0.10	
Large Market Corp Data Rate III	1.80%	$0.10	
Lrg Mkt Corp World Data Rate III	1.80%	$0.10	
Lrg Mkt Corp World Elite DR III	1.80%	$0.10	Business, Corporate, Purchasing, Fleet, Corporate World, Corporate World settlement amounts do not have to match. Provide Tax Amount, Customer of Measure, Extended Item Amount, Debit or Credit Indicator) for all Bu cards that participate in Small Business Spend Processing will qualify for (formally known as Business Enhanced Value) - spend ≥ $25,000 and ~ $ Small Business Spend Processing, Business World transactions will quali Corporate Fleet card at fuel locations are not eligible for this program. Ai Restaurants (5812) merchants are not eligible for this program. Maximum
Business Data Rate III	1.75%	$0.10	
Business Debit Data Rate III	1.80%	$0.10	
Lrg Mkt Purchasing Data Rate III	1.80%	$0.10	
Large Market Fleet Data Rate III	1.80%	$0.10	
Bus Level 2/World Data Rate III	1.91%	$0.10	
Business Level 3/World Elite DR III	1.96%	$0.10	
Business Level 4 Data Rate III	2.06%	$0.10	
Business World Data Rate III	1.91%	$0.10	
Business World Elite Data Rate III	1.96%	$0.10	
Large Market Corporate T&E I	2.70%	$0.00	
Large Market Corp World T&E I	2.70%	$0.00	
Lrg Mkt Corp World Elite T&E I	2.70%	$0.00	
Business T&E I	2.50%	$0.00	Business, Corporate, Purchasing, Fleet, Corporate World, Corporate Wor settlement amounts do not have to match. Eligible Merchants: Airlines (3 (5812). Airline & Passenger Railway require additional General ticket da Processing will qualify for programs based on annual cardholder spend (1 spend ≥ $25,000 and ~ $50,000; Business Level 3 - spend ≥ $50,000 and World transactions will qualify for the Business Level 2 program, and Bu (3000-3299, 4511), 3 days for all other merchants.
Business Debit T&E I	2.50%	$0.00	
Large Market Purchasing T&E I	2.70%	$0.00	
Large Market Fleet T&E I	2.70%	$0.00	
Business Level 2/World T&E I	2.66%	$0.00	
Bus Level 3/World Elite T&E I	2.71%	$0.00	
Business Level 4 T&E I	2.81%	$0.00	
Business World T&E I	2.66%	$0.00	
Business World Elite T&E I	2.71%	$0.00	

Gingergaye Hollowell
www.ElectronicMoneyCompany.com

ATE SCHEDULE (Effective April, 2014)

Transaction Qualification Information

d Elite, Business World, Business World Elite, and Electronic Payment Account cards. Magnetic Swipe required only for Fleet card d settlement amounts do not have to match. Provide Tax Amount & Customer Code (when provided by customer) for all Business & at non-fuel locations. Tax Amount must be between 0.1% to 30% of the sales amount, except for Transportation - Suburban & Local Marinas (4468), Bridge & Road Fees / Tolls (4784), Service Stations (5541), Automated Fuel Dispensers (5542), Convenience Stores 'essional Schools (8220), Charitable Organizations (8398), Religious Organizations (8661), Court Costs / Alimony / Child Support Postal Services - Government (9402), and UK Petrol Stations (9752). Corporate Fleet card (at fuel locations) for fuel and non-fuel iness cards that participate in Small Business Spend Processing will qualify for programs based on annual cardholder spend (reviewed formally known as Business Enhanced Value) - spend≥ $25,000 and ~ $50,000; Business Level 3 - spend ≥ $50,000 and ~ $100,000; mall Business Spend Processing, Business World transactions will qualify for the Business Level 2 program, and Business World Elite -3299, 4511), Vehicle Rental (3351-3500, 7512, 7513, 7519), Lodging (3501-3999, 7011), Passenger Railway (4112), and Restaurants ctions are exempt from timeliness edits. Maximum 3 days to deposit & settle.

Vorld, Business World Elite, Purchasing, and Fleet cards. Magnetic Swipe required only for Fleet card transactions at fuel locations / ave to match. Provide Tax Amount and Customer Code (when provided by customer) for all Business & Corporate card transactions ble Merchants: Marinas (4468), Service Stations (5541), Automated Fuel Dispenser (5542), Convenience Stores (5499), Fuel Dealers timeliness edits. Maximum 3 days to deposit & settle.

ld Elite, Business World, Business World Elite cards. Magnetic Swipe not required / Electronically Authorized. Authorization and r Code (when provided by customer), Corporate line item transaction detail (Product Code, Item Description, Item Quantity, Item Unit iness & Corporate card transactions and for Purchasing and Fleet card transactions at non-fuel locations. Transactions on Business programs based on annual cardholder spend (reviewed quarterly by MasterCard): Business - spend ~ $25,000; Business Level 2 50,000; Business Level 3 - spend ≥ $50,000 and ~ $100,000; Business Level 4 - spend ≥ $100,000. For cards that do not participate in fy for the Business Level 2 program, and Business World Elite transactions will qualify for the Business Level 3 program. MasterCard rlines (3000-3299, 4511), Vehicle Rental (3351-3500, 7512, 7513, 7519), Lodging (3501-3999, 7011), Passenger Railways (4112), and 1 3 days to deposit & settle.

ld Elite, Business World, Business World Elite cards. Magnetic Swipe not required / Electronically Authorized. Authorization and 000-3299, 4511), Vehicle Rental (3351-3500, 7512, 7513, 7519), Lodging (3501-3999, 7011), Passenger Railways (4112), Restaurants ta. Lodging requires Lodging Summary addendum data. Transactions on Business cards that participate in Small Business Spend eviewed quarterly by MasterCard): Business - spend ~ $25,000; Business Level 2 (formally known as Business Enhanced Value) - ~ $100,000; Business Level 4 - spend ≥ $100,000. For cards that do not participate in Small Business Spend Processing, Business isiness World Elite transactions will qualify for the Business Level 3 program. Maximum days to deposit & settle is 9 days for Airlines

Secrets of Credit Card Processing Revealed
www.ElectronicMoneyCompany.com

INTERCHANGE

Program Rate Category	Rates Fee Per Sales $	Per Item	
Large Market Corporate T&E II	2.55%	$0.10	
Large Market Corp World T&E II	2.55%	$0.10	
Lge Mkt Corp World Elite T&E II	2.55%	$0.10	
Business T&E II	2.35%	$0.10	Business, Corporate, Purchasing, Fleet, Corporate World, Corporate Wor
Business Debit T&E II	2.35%	$0.10	settlement amounts do not have to match. Eligible Merchants: Airlines (3
Large Market Purchasing T&E II	2.55%	$0.10	& Passenger Railway require additional General Ticket, Trip Leg, or Rail
Large Market Fleet T&E II	2.55%	$0.10	that participate in Small Business Spend Processing will qualify for prog
Business Level 2/World T&E II	2.51%	$0.10	known as Business Enhanced Value) - spend ≥ $25,000 and ~ $50,000; B
Bus Level 3/World Elite T&E II	2.56%	$0.10	Business Spend Processing, Business World transactions will qualify for
Business Level 4 T&E II	2.66%	$0.10	deposit & settle is 9 days for Airlines (3000-3299, 4511), 3 days for all o
Business World T&E II	2.51%	$0.10	
Business World Elite T&E II	2.56%	$0.10	
Large Market Corporate T&E III	2.50%	$0.10	
Large Market Corp World T&E III	2.50%	$0.10	
Lrg Mkt Corp World Elite T&E III	2.50%	$0.10	
Business T&E III	2.30%	$0.10	
Business Debit T&E III	2.30%	$0.10	Business, Corporate, Purchasing, Fleet, Corporate World, Corporate Wor
Business Debit T&E III Airlines	2.30%	$0.10	settlement amounts do not have to match. Eligible Merchants: Airlines (3
Large Market Purchasing T&E III	2.50%	$0.10	& Passenger Railways require additional General Ticket, Trip Leg, or Ra
Large Market Fleet T&E III	2.50%	$0.10	that participate in Small Business Spend Processing will qualify for prog
Large Market T&E III Airlines	2.43%	$0.10	known as Business Enhanced Value) - spend ≥ $25,000 and ~ $50,000; B
Business Level 2/World T&E III	2.46%	$0.10	Business Spend Processing, Business World transactions will qualify for
Bus Level 3/World Elite T&E III	2.51%	$0.10	deposit & settle is 9 days for Airlines (3000-3299, 4511), 3 days for all o
Business Level 4 T&E III	2.61%	$0.10	
Business World T&E III	2.46%	$0.10	
Business World Elite T&E III	2.51%	$0.10	
Large Market Corporate Standard	2.95%	$0.10	
Large Market Corp World Standard	2.95%	$0.10	
Lrg Mkt Corp World Elite Standard	2.95%	$0.10	
Business Standard	2.95%	$0.10	Business, Corporate, Purchasing, Fleet, Corporate World, Corporate Wor
Business Debit Standard	2.95%	$0.10	required. Transactions on Business cards that participate in Small Busine
Business Level 2/World Standard	3.11%	$0.10	spend ~ $25,000; Business Level 2 (formally known as Business Enhanc
Bus Level 3/World Elite Standard	3.16%	$0.10	For cards that do not participate in Small Business Spend Processing, Bu
Business Level 4 Standard	3.26%	$0.10	Business Level 3 program. Maximum 30 days to deposit & settle.
Business World Standard	3.11%	$0.10	
Business World Elite Standard	3.16%	$0.10	
Interregional Electronic	1.95%	$0.00	Consumer cards issued in any region, Premium (Platinum and Titanium
			Prepaid Platinum Travel cards issued in the LAC region, and World card
			Black Edition and World Debit Embossed cards issued in Europe, and W
Interregional Premium Electronic	2.70%	$0.00	code of the cardholder. Face-to-Face / Magnetic Stripe Read / Signature
			settlement amounts can differ up to 10% (up to 25% for Beauty and Barb
			(5813), Fast Food (5814), Lodging (3501-3999 or 7011), Vehicle Rental
Interregional Super Premium Electronic	2.83%	$0.00	Authorization and settlement amounts do not have to match for Platinum
			5962, 5964, 5965, 5966, 5967, 5968, 5969) merchants not eligible for thi
Interregional Standard	2.45%	$0.00	Consumer cards issued in any region, Premium (Platinum and Titanium
			Prepaid Platinum Travel cards issued in the LAC region, and World card
Interregional Premium Standard	2.70%	$0.00	Black Edition and World Debit Embossed cards issued in Europe, and W
IR Super Premium Standard	2.83%	$0.00	code of the cardholder. Transaction date more than 5 days old. Maximun

Gingergaye Hollowell
www.ElectronicMoneyCompany.com

RATE SCHEDULE   (Effective April, 2014)

Transaction Qualification Information

ld Elite, Business World, Business World Elite cards. Magnetic Swipe not required. Electronically Authorized. Authorization and
000-3299, 4511), Vehicle Rental (3351-3500, 7512, 7513, 7519), Lodging (3501-3999, 7011), and Passenger Railways (4112). Airline
l data. Vehicle Rental require Rental Detail data. Lodging requires Lodging summary addendum data. Transactions on Business cards
rams based on annual cardholder spend (reviewed quarterly by MasterCard): Business - spend ~ $25,000; Business Level 2 (formally
usiness Level 3 - spend ≥ $50,000 and ~ $100,000; Business Level 4 - spend ≥ $100,000. For cards that do not participate in Small
the Business Level 2 program, and Business World Elite transactions will qualify for the Business Level 3 program. Maximum days to
ther merchants.

ld Elite, Business World, Business World Elite cards. Magnetic Swipe not required / Electronically Authorized. Authorization and
000-3299, 4511), Vehicle Rental (3351-3500, 7512, 7513, 7519), Lodging (3501-3999, 7011), and Passenger Railways (4112). Airline
il data. Vehicle Rental require Rental Detail data. Lodging requires Lodging summary addendum data. Transactions on Business cards
rams based on annual cardholder spend (reviewed quarterly by MasterCard): Business - spend ~ $25,000; Business Level 2 (formally
usiness Level 3 - spend ≥ $50,000 and ~ $100,000; Business Level 4 - spend ≥ $100,000. For cards that do not participate in Small
the Business Level 2 program, and Business World Elite transactions will qualify for the Business Level 3 program. Maximum days to
ther merchants.

rld Elite, Business World, Business World Elite, and Electronic Payment Account cards. Magnetic swipe not required / Authorization
ss Spend Processing will qualify for programs based on annual cardholder spend (reviewed quarterly by MasterCard): Business -
ed Value) - spend≥ $25,000 and ~ $50,000, Business Level 3 - spend ≥ $50,000 and ~ $100,000; Business Level 4 - spend ≥ $100,000.
siness World transactions will qualify for the Business Level 2 program, and Business World Elite transactions will qualify for the

cards issued in the Asia Pacific, SAMEA, and LAC regions, Platinum cards issued in Europe, World Elite cards issued in Canada,
is issued in the U.S.), and Super Premium (World and Black cards issued in the Asia Pacific, Europe, LAC, and SAMEA regions, World
/orld Elite cards issued in the U.S., Asia Pacific, and SAMEA regions) where the country code of the merchant differs from the country
Obtained / Electronically Authorized. Key-entered transactions not eligible for this program. For Consumer cards only, authorization and
er Shops - 7230 for transactions up to $25). Authorization and settlement amounts do not have to match for Restaurants (5812), Bars
(3351-3500, 7512, 7513, 7519), Airlines (3000-3299, 4511), Cruise Line / Steamship (4411), and Passenger Railways (4112).
, World, World Elite, and Black transactions for all merchants. Automated Fuel Dispenser (5542) and Mail / Telephone Order (5960,
is program. Maximum 5 days to deposit & settle. Rate includes the MasterCard Acquirer Program Support Fee.

cards issued in the Asia Pacific, SAMEA, and LAC regions, Platinum cards issued in Europe, World Elite cards issued in Canada,
is issued in the U.S.), and Super Premium (World and Black cards issued in the Asia Pacific, Europe, LAC, and SAMEA regions, World
/orld Elite cards issued in the U.S., Asia Pacific, and SAMEA regions) where the country code of the merchant differs from the country
n 30 days to deposit & settle. Rate includes the MasterCard Acquirer Program Support Fee.

Secrets of Credit Card Processing Revealed
www.ElectronicMoneyCompany.com

INTERCHANGE R

Program Rate Category	Rates Fee Per Sales $	Per Item	
Interregional Electronic Consumer	1.95%	$0.00	Electronic Consumer Cards. Face-to-Face / Magnetic Stripe Read / Signat can differ up to 10% (up to 25% for Beauty and Barber Shops - 7230 for t (5814), Lodging (3501-3999 or 7011), Vehicle Rental (3351-3500, 7512, Dispensers (5542) and Mail / Telephone Order (5960, 5962, 5964, 5965, Program Support Fee.
Interregional Electronic Corporate	2.70%	$0.00	Electronic Corporate Cards. Face-to-Face / Magnetic Stripe Read / Signat Automated Fuel Dispensers (5542) not eligible for this program. Maximu
Regulated Debit - U.S. Territory	0.90%	$0.21	Regulated Consumer and Commercial Debit and Prepaid Cards identified Territory issued cards at a U.S. merchant location or U.S. issued cards at Islands. Issuer has NOT certified its fraud prevention procedures. Rate In Rate includes MasterCard Acquirer Program Support Fee.
Regulated Debit with Fraud Adjustment - U.S. Territory	0.90%	$0.22	Regulated Consumer and Commercial Debit and Prepaid Cards identified Territory issued cards at a U.S. merchant location or U.S. issued cards at Islands. Issuer has certified its fraud prevention procedures. Rate Indicato deposit & settle. Rate includes MasterCard Acquirer Program Support Fe
Regulated Debit Small Ticket - US Territory	0.90%	$0.21	Regulated Consumer and Commercial Debit and Prepaid Cards identified Territory issued cards at a U.S. merchant location or U.S. issued cards at Islands. Rate Indicator value identified by Issuers and Card Organizations
Regulated Debit Small Ticket with Fraud Adjustment - US Territory	0.90%	$0.22	Fast Food Restaurants (5814) and Videotape Rental Stores (7841). Autho Program Support Fee.
Interregional Purchasing Data Rate II	2.55%	$0.00	Purchasing or Fleet Cards, and Electronic Payment Accounts (at non-fuel do not have to match. Provide sales Tax Amount and Customer Code (wh Stations (5541), Automated Fuel Dispensers (5542), Convenience Stores Acquirer Program Support Fee.
Interregional Purchasing Large Ticket	1.75%	$30.00	Purchasing or Fleet Cards, and Electronic Payment Accounts issued in a Airlines (3000-3299, 4511), Vehicle Rental (3351-3500, 7512, 7513, 751 deposit & settle. Rate includes the MasterCard Acquirer Program Suppor
Interregional Purchasing	2.85%	$0.00	Purchasing or Fleet Cards, and Electronic Payment Accounts issued in a
Interregional Corporate	2.85%	$0.00	Business, Corporate, and Premium Commercial (Platinum, World, World
Interregional Premium Commercial	2.85%	$0.00	Program Support Fee.
Interregional UCAF - Full	2.39%	$0.00	Consumer cards issued in any region. Premium (Platinum and Titanium Prepaid Platinum Travel cards issued in the LAC region, and World card
Interregional Premium UCAF - Full	2.70%	$0.00	Black Edition and World Debit Embossed cards issued in Europe, and W code of the cardholder. Applies to all intra and inter regional transactions
I/R Super Premium UCAF - Full	2.83%	$0.00	participation in MasterCard UCAF. UCAF indicator of 2 must be present 5 days to deposit & settle. Rate includes the MasterCard Acquirer Progra
Interregional UCAF – Merchant	2.29%	$0.00	Consumer cards issued in any region. Premium (Platinum and Titanium Prepaid Platinum Travel cards issued in the LAC region, and World card
Interregional Premium UCAF - Merchant	2.70%	$0.00	Black Edition and World Debit Embossed cards issued in Europe, and W code of the cardholder. Applies to all intra and inter regional transactions participation in MasterCard UCAF. UCAF indicator of 1 must be present
I/R Super Premium UCAF - Merch	2.83%	$0.00	days to deposit & settle. Rate includes the MasterCard Acquirer Program
International Payment Transaction	1.04%	$0.53	Consumer and Corporate cards only. Applies to all intra and inter region not have to match. Eligible Merchants: Payment Service Provider - Mem
International Corporate Payment Transaction	1.04%	$0.53	the MasterCard Acquirer Program Support Fee.
Assessments	0.11%	$0.00	Fee assessed on the gross dollar amount of all MasterCard transactions.

Gingergaye Hollowell
www.ElectronicMoneyCompany.com

ATE SCHEDULE (Effective April, 2014)

Transaction Qualification Information

ure Obtained / Electronically Authorized. Key-entered transactions not eligible for this program. Authorization and settlement amounts ransactions up to $25). Authorization and settlement amounts do not have to match for Restaurants (5812), Bars (5813), Fast Food 7513, 7519), Airlines (3000-3299, 4511), Cruise Line / Steamship (4411), and Passenger Railways, (4112). Automated Fuel 5966, 5967, 5968, 5969) not eligible for this program. Maximum 5 days to deposit & settle. Rate includes the MasterCard Acquirer

ure Obtained / Electronically Authorized. Authorization and settlement amounts do not have to match. Key-entered transactions and m 30 days to deposit & settle. Rate includes the MasterCard Acquirer Program Support Fee.

by Issuers and Card Organizations as being subject to the June 29, 2011 Federal Reserve final rule on Debit Card interchange. U.S. a U.S. Territory location. U.S. Territories include American Samoa, Guam, Northern Mariana Islands, Puerto Rico, and U.S. Virgin dicator value identified by Issuers and Card Organizations of B (Base). Authorization required. Maximum 30 days to deposit & settle.

by Issuers and Card Organizations as being subject to the June 29, 2011 Federal Reserve final rule on Debit Card interchange. U.S. a U.S. Territory location. U.S. Territories include American Samoa, Guam, Northern Mariana Islands, Puerto Rico, and U.S. Virgin r value identified by Issuers and Card Organizations of 1 (Base plus Fraud Adjustment). Authorization required. Maximum 30 days to e.

by Issuers and Card Organizations as being subject to the June 29, 2011 Federal Reserve final rule on Debit Card interchange. U.S. a U.S. Territory location. U.S. Territories include American Samoa, Guam, Northern Mariana Islands, Puerto Rico, and U.S. Virgin of S (Regulated Small Ticket Base). Transaction amount $10.00 or less / Card Present / Electronically Authorized. Eligible Merchants: rization and settlement amounts do not have to match. Maximum 2 days to deposit & settle. Rate includes MasterCard Acquirer

locations) issued in a foreign country. Magnetic swipe not required / Electronically Authorized. Authorization and settlement amounts en provided by the customer). Tax Amount must be between 0.1% to 30% of the sales amount, except for Marinas (4468), Service (5499), Fuel Dealers (5983), and UK Petrol Stations (9752). Maximum 5 days to deposit & settle. Rate includes the MasterCard

foreign country. Magnetic swipe not required / Electronically Authorized. Authorization and settlement amounts do not have to match. 9), Lodging (3501-3999, 7011), Passenger Railways (4112), and Restaurants (5812) not eligible for this program. Maximum 30 days to t Fee.

foreign country. Maximum 30 days to deposit & settle. Rate includes the MasterCard Acquirer Program Support Fee.

l Elite, and Black) cards issued in a foreign country. Maximum 30 days to deposit & settle. Rate includes the MasterCard Acquirer

ards issued in the Asia Pacific, SAMEA, and LAC regions, Platinum cards issued in Europe, World Elite cards issued in Canada, s issued in the U.S.), and Super Premium (World and Black cards issued in the Asia Pacific, Europe, LAC, and SAMEA regions, World orld Elite cards issued in the U.S., Asia Pacific, and SAMEA regions) where the country code of the merchant differs from the country except for U.S. Region and Canada Region. Terminal type must indicate Electronic Commerce Transactions and merchant and issuer's . Magnetic swipe not required / Electronically Authorized. Authorization and settlement amounts do not have to match. Maximum in Support Fee.

ards issued in the Asia Pacific, SAMEA, and LAC regions, Platinum cards issued in Europe, World Elite cards issued in Canada, s issued in the U.S.), and Super Premium (World and Black cards issued in the Asia Pacific, Europe, LAC, and SAMEA regions, World orld Elite cards issued in the U.S., Asia Pacific, and SAMEA regions) where the country code of the merchant differs from the country except for U.S. Region and Canada Region. Terminal type must indicate Electronic Commerce Transactions and merchant's . Magnetic swipe not required / Electronically Authorized. Authorization and settlement amounts do not have to match. Maximum 5 Support Fee.

l transactions except for U.S. Region and Canada Region. Magnetic Stripe Read not required. Authorization and settlement amounts do ber Financial Institution (6532) and Payment Service Provider - Merchant (6533). Maximum 30 days to deposit and settle. Rate includes

Secrets of Credit Card Processing Revealed
www.ElectronicMoneyCompany.com

INTERCHANGE

Program Rate Category	Rates		
	Fee Per Sales $	Per Item	
Assessments (>=$1,000)	0.02%	$0.00	Fee assessed on the gross dollar amount of MasterCard Consumer and Co...
Account Status Inquiry Fee - Intraregional	0.00%	$0.025	Fee assessed on all Account Status Inquiry Service messages where the c... submitted for $0 and are used to validate cardholder account numbers and...
Account Status Inquiry Fee - Interregional	0.00%	$0.03	Fee assessed on all Account Status Inquiry Service messages where the c... submitted for $0 and are used to validate cardholder account numbers and...
Card Validation Code 2 (CVC 2) Fee	0.00%	$0.0025	Fee assessed on all authorizations that include Card Validation Code 2 (C... the screening tools used by merchants to ensure that the person placing th...
Processing Integrity Fee	0.00%	$0.055	Fee assessed on all MasterCard authorized transactions which are not foll... Dispensers (5542) not subject to this fee. Rate includes additional $0.01 r...
License Volume Fee	0.0050%	$0.00	Fee assessed on the gross dollar amount of all MasterCard transactions (c... licensing and third party processing.

Gingergaye Hollowell
www.ElectronicMoneyCompany.com

RATE SCHEDULE (Effective April, 2014)

Transaction Qualification Information

mmercial credit transactions that are $1,000 or greater.

ountry code of the merchant is the same as the country code of the cardholder. Account Status Inquiry Service transactions must be
l other elements, such as CVC2 and AVS, prior to obtaining an actual authorization.

ountry code of the merchant is different from the country code of the cardholder. Account Status Inquiry Service transactions must be
l other elements, such as CVC2 and AVS, prior to obtaining an actual authorization.

VC 2) validation. CVC 2 is an optional service from MasterCard that was implemented to help reduce the risk of fraud and is part of
e order has the card. Does not apply to Account Status Inquiry transactions.

owed by a matching MasterCard clearing transaction (or not reversed in the case of a cancelled transaction). Automated Fuel
eporting cost from MasterCard for each transaction. Billed on a one month lag.

redit and signature debit). Fee based on a good faith effort to recover and allocate among all customers MasterCard's annual fees for

Secrets of Credit Card Processing Revealed
www.ElectronicMoneyCompany.com

Visa® and MasterCard® Credit Vo

This Credit Voucher Programs and Rate Schedule contains a summary of the primary qualification criteria established
conflict, the interchange requirements established by the Card Organizations (sometimes referred to associations) will

Program Rate Category	Rates		
	Per Sales $	Per Item	
MASTERCARD**			
Consumer Credit			
CONS CR RF 1	2.42%	$0.00	World MasterCard, High Value World Ma 3500, 7512, 7513, 7519), Cruise Lines / St Agencies (4722).
CONS CR RF 2	2.09%	$0.00	Mail Order (5960, 5962, 5964-5969) and T Fuel Dealers (5983), excluding World Mas
CONS CR RF 3	1.95%	$0.00	Drug Stores, Education, Professional Servi World Elite MasterCard transactions at Re World MasterCard, and World Elite Maste
CONS CR RF 4	1.82%	$0.00	Clothing Stores, Discount Stores, Gas Stat MasterCard, High Value World MasterCar
CONS CR RF 5	1.73%	$0.00	Department Stores, Electronic / Appliance MasterCard, High Value World MasterCar
Consumer Debit			
CONS DB RF 1	1.72%	$0.00	All industries, except Airlines (3000-3299 Issuers and Card Organizations as being su
CONS DB RF 2	1.68%	$0.00	Airlines (3000-3299, 4511) and Passenger Organizations as being subject to the June
CONS DB RF 3	1.40%	$0.00	All industries except Mail Order (5960, 59 Debit and Prepaid Cards identified by Issu not eligible for this rate.
Commercial Credit			
CORP CR RF 1	2.37%	$0.00	Discount Stores, Drug Stores, Food Stores
CORP CR RF 2	2.30%	$0.00	Car Rental, Clothing Stores, Education, H
CORP CR RF 3	2.21%	$0.00	Airlines, Hardware, Healthcare, Mail Ord
CORP CR RF 4	2.16%	$0.00	Department Stores, Electronic / Appliance

****Credit (or sales return) transactions for regulated signature debit and interregional transactions are applied back agai
Commercial Debit and Prepaid transactions identified by Issuers and Card Organizations as being subject to the June 2

Gingergaye Hollowell
www.ElectronicMoneyCompany.com

ucher Programs and Rate Schedule (Effective April, 2014)

by Visa and MasterCard for most interchange programs - it is not all inclusive. In the event of any ambiguity or determine the interchange programs at which your transactions qualify.

Transaction Qualification Information

sterCard, and World Elite MasterCard transactions at T&E merchants: Airlines (3000-3299, 4511), Car Rental (3351- eamship (4411), Hotel / Motel (3501-3999, 7011), Passenger Railway (4112), Restaurants (5812), and Travel

elecommunications (4812, 4814, 4816, 4821), Cable & Satellite TV (4899), Travel Agencies (4722), Utilities (4900), sterCard, High Value World MasterCard, and World Elite MasterCard transactions.

ices, Recreation, Repair Shops, Restaurant / Bars (excluding World MasterCard, High Value World MasterCard, and staurants - 5812), and Other Services and Airlines (3000-3299, 4511), excluding World MasterCard, High Value rCard transactions.

ions, Hardware, Healthcare, Sporting Goods & Toy Stores, and Other Retail and Other Transport (excluding World d, and World Elite MasterCard cards at Passenger Railways - 4112 and Cruise Lines - 4411).

Stores, Food Stores / Warehouse, Interior Furnishings, Vehicles, and Quasi Cash and Hotel / Motel, excluding World d, and World Elite MasterCard transactions.

, 4511) and Passenger Railways (4112). Regulated Consumer and Commercial Debit and Prepaid Cards identified by ibject to the June 29, 2011 Federal Reserve final rule on Debit Card interchange not eligible for this rate.

Railways (4112). Regulated Consumer and Commercial Debit and Prepaid Cards identified by Issuers and Card 29, 2011 Federal Reserve final rule on Debit Card interchange not eligible for this rate.

'62, 5964-5969), Airlines (3000-3299, 4511), and Passenger Railways (4112). Regulated Consumer and Commercial ers and Card Organizations as being subject to the June 29, 2011 Federal Reserve final rule on Debit Card interchange

/ Warehouse, Quasi Cash, Recreation, Restaurant / Bars, Utilities, and Other Transport.

otel / Motel, Repair Shops, Sporting Goods & Toy Stores, Travel Agencies, and Vehicles.

r, Other Retail, Other Services, and Professional Services.

Stores, Gas Stations, and Interior Furnishings.

nst the interchange program for which the purchase transaction originally qualified. Regulated Consumer and 9, 2011 Federal Reserve final rule on Debit Card interchange.

Understanding the Interchange Chart

1. If you study the chart, you can see that **different industries are charged different interchange rates**. For example, hotel, restaurant, retail, fuel, and groceries all have their own categories of rates. The lower the rate, the lower the risk of chargeback for that industry. So if you

are in retail, you get a different rate than if you are in the restaurant business.

2. **The rate for a credit card is different than the rate for a debit card run as a credit card, and a regulated debit card has a different rate than a non-regulated debit card.**

The determination of regulated or non-regulated was created by the Durbin Act. Basically it was decided by Senator Durbin and his committee and later adopted by Congress that the big banks like Bank of America and Wells Fargo would be restricted as far as how much they could collect in debit card interchange fees from merchants accepting their customers' debit cards. The smaller banks were not going to be restricted on the fees they wanted to collect.

So, as a merchant, when you take a debit card issued by one of the big banks it should not cost you as much as taking a card issued by a small credit union, provided you are set up on a cost plus program (explained under *Processor Surcharge* later in this chapter). This is good news for merchants, especially when about 70% of all debit cards are issued by big banks. The interesting part is that your processor may not be passing this savings on to you. They may be keeping it for themselves.

They have to make money somewhere in order to provide their service. By being educated, you get to know exactly what they are charging you and where. This gives you power in negotiating that surcharge.

By the way, a debit card run with a pin number is processed through a completely different network with different rates. See addendum C.

3. Another differentiation of rate is over **whether the card is swiped, keyed into a terminal from a phone order, or taken over the internet or a mobile gateway**. The risk of a charge back is higher when the card is not present. Therefore, the rate is lower when the card is swiped.

4. **Address verification**, if performed, lowers the risk of taking a fraudulent card and therefore lowers the interchange rate. This is controlled by the merchant at the point of sale. If your employees can't be bothered entering the address and zip code or they don't ask the customer for the information, you will pay a higher rate for the transaction. The idea is that if the customer you are talking to over the phone has their real card, they know the billing address of the card. When someone is using a stolen card to purchase over the phone or the internet, they do not know the address.

5. **Commercial and business cards have a higher risk of fraudulent use,** therefore their rates are higher. Different types of business cards have different rates. However, if you collect more information about the transaction such as sales, tax, shipping info, and purchase order number, the interchange is significantly lower than if you don't take the time to enter that information. Usually this information requires a gateway as opposed to a credit card terminal to process. See the section on B2B processing with detailed information for merchants taking commercial cards and discover the huge savings possible if you take payments from other businesses!

Understanding The Processor's Surcharge

The processor has to charge money on top of the interchange fees in order to get paid for providing a service: transferring the money from your card to your bank account, monitoring for fraud, customer service regarding your merchant account, and equipment or gateway.

There are a few different ways the processor surcharges the interchange cost.

1. **Cost plus a percentage and/or a transaction amount**. As you may have noticed on the interchange chart, there is a percentage rate and a transaction fee in the rate structure. That is to even out the variance in an average ticket. On a small fast food ticket, the percentage does not amount to enough surcharge and the transaction fee surcharge is necessary. On a large ticket, the transaction fee surcharge does not give the processor enough for his time and service, so the percentage is more of a factor.

    This method is simple to understand provided the merchant understands the interchange chart. At the same time, there will be many different charges for all the different types of cards that come across as payments and can be a bit unpredictable or seem confusing to the merchant. There are huge advantages to a merchant who takes lots of debit cards when they are on a cost plus program versus a tiered program, explained below. The cost of a regulated debit card is .05% plus $.22. Tiered pricing often charges merchants 1.75% plus $.25 for these types of debit cards, yielding huge profits for the processor. More information on debit savings from cost plus is explained in chapter five.

2. **Tiered pricing** throws all transactions in three buckets with only three rates to be concerned about. One bucket is for swiped transactions, one for keyed transactions and rewards cards, and a third for business cards or keyed-in rewards cards. This pricing system allows for an easy to understand merchant statement. However, generally the processor is charging a slightly higher surcharge than with cost plus. The processor has to make sure he has his buckets covered for all the scenarios of rates. Tiered pricing gives the advantage to the processor. Interchange Cost Plus pricing gives the advantage to the merchant.

    Some processors have an expanded variation of tiered pricing with six or more buckets. They add more separated buckets for swiped rewards cards, keyed-in rewards cards, swiped debit cards, and keyed-in debit cards. They can even get more creative than that.

3. **Bill-back pricing** is a combination of cost plus and tiered. It provides for cost plus pricing for swiped cards, but then extra is charged for keyed-in cards, rewards cards, and corporate cards. This pricing formula is most confusing to merchants and therefore allows for trickery in padding the surcharges.

4. **Flat fee pricing** allows the merchant to have the same fee for every transaction. This makes it easy for

the merchant to monitor and budget. However, it removes the burden from the merchant's practice to keep the interchange costs lower by always doing address verification or entering business card data such as order number and sales tax. As a result, the processor needs to protect its profitable surcharge and may feel it necessary to cover those situations with a higher overall rate. For merchants who don't take business cards or over the phone transactions, this concern does not exist.

Chapter Four

The So-Called "Hidden Fees"

Besides interchange costs and transaction fees, there are a myriad of other fees. Many times salespeople don't address all the details and merchants are left wondering about all the other so-called "hidden fees."

1. Some of these fees are Visa and MasterCard fees called **"Pass Thru" Fees.** There is nothing anyone can do about these. They are fixed costs and everybody has to pay them. They have names such as Acquired Fee, International Fee, NABU Fee, Data Fee, Base Trans Fee, Border Fee, etc.

2. **Monthly fee**, also called Statement Fee, On File Fee, Monthly Service Fee, and the like. Use your imagination to come up with a bunch of different names for charging a fee to keep a merchant account open. This fee covers the cost of all the technical support and customer service people that answer phone calls. Every processor has this cost and, therefore, this fee. It usually varies between $5/month and $20/month. Sometimes a processor has two fees to make it look smaller.

3. **PCI compliance fee** is mandated by the industry. All processors need to monitor whether merchants are protecting the credit card information of customers. In this day and age, there are few bank robberies and a lot of credit card fraud. We all need to do our part to protect against fraud in this digital age, which is a huge convenience and benefit to us all. This fee ranges from $90 per year to $195 per year depending on whether you use an analog terminal, digital

terminal, or a gateway. The gateways and digital terminal lines need to be scanned for viruses gathering credit card data, therefore the PCI compliance fee is higher. This fee might also appear as a monthly fee with the same price divided by 12. In addition, each merchant is required to fill out a compliance survey annually. Processors notify merchants of this annual requirement on their merchant statement; however, many merchants miss seeing it. When the merchant neglects to do the annual survey, the processor adds on a monthly fee varying from $19.95/month to $70/month. It is a slap on the wrist to get your attention. Usually it works quite well and the merchant cries ouch and gets his survey done.

4. **Club fee, maintenance service fee,** or other various similar names is a fee to cover free paper supplies and free terminal replacement.

5. **Batch fees** are transaction fees for sending daily batch total information.

6. **Annual fees** are extra fees a processor can build into his surcharge.

7. **Early termination fee** is a fee imposed on a merchant for terminating their service before the end of a contract. Some processors will waive this fee. Others feel that they need some assurance that they get some money should a new merchant close his business shortly after opening it or switch to a different

processor before the current processor can recoup their costs of setting up a merchant. Many processors use this fee to deter their merchants from switching processors.

Chapter Five

General Guidelines By Industry

B2B (Business to Business) versus B2C (Business to Consumer) Payment Processing

"Level 2" Processing

It is virtually unknown to B2B merchants that they can **save on average a huge .5%** on a B2B transaction (payment transaction from another business) simply by entering sales tax and the order number into their terminal or gateway! This is called level two processing and both terminals and gateways can be set up to prompt for this second level of information. By passing this information to the Visa/MasterCard networks, the transaction is considered much lower risk and therefore carries a lower interchange rate. The request for level two processing needs to be handled with the processor at application time so that the software loaded into the terminal or gateway can be built properly to prompt for the information. This is the first place where many processors fail to support their B2B client. The salesman may not be trained in level two processing. The processor's surcharge is unaffected, therefore the processor may not be motivated to pass on this information to their sales people or their merchants.

At the time of transaction, it is up to the merchant (in most cases, the merchant's employee) to answer the prompts and enter in the correct sales tax and an order number (any number qualifies as an order number). If the employee chooses to skip this process by tabbing through it, the transaction is considered higher risk and qualifies at a higher interchange rate, costing the business owner more money.

"Level 3" Processing

Transactions from Purchasing Cards

Larger businesses with multiple employees have purchasing cards for employees that do not require a requisition form or supervisory sign-off. It is a way to give employees authority to purchase items on an expense account. The business then tracks the purchases internally. They do this with a pooled purchasing credit card, differentiated from a business credit card, usually owned by a small business owner who only has a card for himself to track business expenses.

Many merchants who take credit card payments from other businesses or corporations regularly deal with these types of cards. The issuing banks have lower risk when extra data is passed back to the owner of the purchasing card such as sales tax, purchase order, shipping information, commodity code information, and other item details. Therefore the interchange cost associated with accepting a purchasing card varies from **1.5% to 3%** depending on the data passed along. This can easily amount to **savings of $500 to $1000 per month**.

Again, many credit card processing sales people are totally unaware of how to save their clients money with these types of cards. They spend most of their time calling on retail or restaurant merchants who process large numbers of cards and don't take purchasing cards. They have a script for generic sales calls. As a result, B2B merchants are underserved by the credit card processing industry. It behooves this type of merchant to talk to a credit card processing salesperson knowledgeable in this area because **saving 1.5% is HUGE**! It amounts to over $500 per month for even a small B2B merchant processing $35,000 per month. Large B2B merchants processing $100,000 a month save a whopping $1,500 per month. Sometimes B2B merchants take single large payment amounts like $50,000 for just one purchase, and if they learn to take the card properly and enter the extra data, they save $750 on just that one purchase. The interesting thing is that the under-educated credit card salesperson does not make more or less money by serving the B2B merchant because the savings are all in the interchange cost. Surcharge is not affected.

Most B2B merchants can spare a few more seconds to enter this information into their gateway to take advantage of these huge savings. They are not taking cards from people standing in a line where speed is of the essence. There are some tricks to entering this detailed information into their gateway. Get with a processor who specializes in this area for the best benefit!

My business, **Electronic Money Company**, is a unique service provider of credit card processing because we are **Interchange Management Experts.** We offer the added service of an "Interchange Management Audit," showing merchants **on average $500 to $1000 savings** per month with this service.

- We set up our merchants on Interchange Cost Plus.
- We provide a monthly audit of a merchant's card processing statement.
- We provide a report revealing transactions that could have qualified at a lower rate, but did not.
- We report back to the merchant monthly what could have been done to lower their interchange rate.
- We provide repeated FREE training to merchants and their employees.

To read more about this valuable Interchange Management service, go to www.ElectronicMoneyCompany.com.

Small Tickets (Convenience Stores or Fast Food)

This type of merchant should be most concerned about their transaction fee, the surcharge transaction fee from the processor. A percentage rate is an insignificant factor since the average ticket is small. Most of the transactions will be swiped with the customer present, and most swiped transactions will be debit cards.

A significant factor for these types of merchants would be to go with a cost plus program where you can get regulated debit rates. The regulated debit rate for debit cards issued by large institutional banks is .05% plus $.22 compared to the non-regulated debit rate of .80% plus $.15. If you are a fast food location, convenience store, or a retail store with low average tickets and your processor is charging you a tiered rate, you are not getting **the lower interchange rate of debit cards and the even lower rate of regulated debit cards!**

Fine Dining Restaurants

You will want to consider both the rate and transaction fee in your analysis of card fees. Your transactions are all swiped. You will be taking lots of debit cards, rewards cards, plus corporate cards because business people like to entertain. You do not have any extra opportunities to improve the interchange rates by the way you take your cards because you are already swiping them. You will simply want to please your customers by taking whatever cards your customers want to use.

Hotels

Again, you will be swiping cards and taking a lot of corporate cards. It is imperative that if you have customers who have varied lengths of stay that you use a POS or a terminal with check-in and check-out functionality to get the best rates. If most of your customers simply stay one or two nights, then a simple retail merchant account will suffice and serve you well.

Professional Services such as Contractors

Here the ability to swipe a card in the field can save you a ton of money versus calling in to an office. There is a big difference in interchange cost between the swiped rate and the keyed-in rate. There are all sorts of options for taking cards with mobile phones nowadays. Additionally, there are POS mobile systems, which track inventory sold in the field integrated to a POS system in the office.

Retail with the Customer Present

Many of your transactions are debit and many are rewards. A cost plus program will work best for you to take advantage of regulated debit rates.

Retail with the Customer Not Present

Pay attention to address verification as you key-in transactions from the phone or internet.

Chapter Six

Value Added Merchant Services

Payment Processing Equipment

Processors are typically your source for terminals, e-commerce gateways, and POS equipment. The equipment can be purchased outright or with a lease to buy.

Terminals are moving to the new EMV technology. EMV stands for EuroMasterCardVisa. It represents new technology now coming to the United States that has been prevalent in Europe for several years. The technology involves a chip embedded in the credit card which holds the cardholder's information. This technology is much more secure and prevents fraud better than the old mag stripe technology. It does so because the chip attaches a unique cryptogram to the card transaction. This technology makes it much more difficult for a fraudster to copy someone's credit card and make a duplicate card. The technology will be required in new credit cards that are issued.

Merchants will be required to update their hardware and software to read EMV cards. You will also notice the changes in ATM machines. Merchants will be strongly encouraged to invest in new equipment and start using EMV-capable terminals and swipers with the new technology starting in October of 2015. The strong encouragement will involve a shift in the liability of processing a fraudulent card. A merchant who inadvertently takes a fraudulent credit card payment with a mag stripe terminal, not EMV capable, will have to eat the transaction unconditionally. This is a shift from the way it is handled currently, where Visa and MasterCard and the issuing bank carries that liability. Basically it will be financially burdensome *not* to invest in the new hardware and/or software after October 2015.

Point of Sale (POS)

Technological development is motivating merchants toward Point of Sale systems and away from credit card terminals sitting next to a cash register. The cost of a POS is so reasonable and there is an additional savings in efficiency and time when the cash register and credit card terminal are integrated into one system. The cash, credit cards, and checks are automatically reconciled together in a Point of Sale computer, saving management time reconciling the credit card terminal to the cash register at the end of every day. It goes without saying that reconciling can detect missing cash and transactions. The easy reconciliation also saves a minimum of 30 minutes per day. Translated into cost savings, even if you only figure management time at $20/hour, the savings is $10 per day times 30 days, amounting to $300 per month.

Another advantage of a POS is that it will track inventory going in and out of the business via purchases. Counting, tracking, and reconciling inventory with a POS system prevents inventory theft. Besides inventory reports, a myriad of other reports are available for management at the touch of a button, yielding information regarding profitability, bestselling hours of the day, details of products sold, and which ones sell the most and return the highest profit. Payroll can be tracked in a POS, saving hours of bookkeeping time, along with employee scheduling. The POS can also manage a database of customer information, the most valuable asset of the business. It is the marketing value of this database to a future owner that escalates the sales price of a business.

Some POS software can also be integrated with marketing software, automatically reaching out to customers via email, text messaging, and direct mail. A POS can replace a human in its efficiency, saving the owner not only dollars but valuable time which he can then spend with his family. The ROI is enormous in terms of profitability.

Gift and Loyalty Cards

Gift and loyalty card processing is another valuable marketing tool provided by processors. It can be added to credit card terminals, POS systems, and online e-commerce sites. Gift cards are popular products for consumers to purchase and give merchants the opportunity to gain new customers. Loyalty cards give point or dollar value for customer loyalty. Points can be added for frequency of visits or as a percentage of purchases. Data can be gathered on customer purchasing preferences and marketing can be pushed out to build even more customer loyalty. It costs seven times more to get a new customer than it does to get a current customer to come back and purchase again. In reality, if a business could put a fence around a core group who purchase again and again, it does not need to rely on getting more customers to come in. A loyalty card program does just that.

Financing - Advance Funding

Financing of advances on credit card processing receivables have become popular in recent times. Many times a business needs a sum of money to take advantage of a discounted volume purchase of product from a vendor. Other times a business may be looking to expand their square footage in order to generate more sales. Finding this money from banks can be time consuming and costly. An advance on credit card receivables is quick to secure, only takes a few days to get funded, and is also quick to pay off.

Another method of financing available from merchant service providers are lease purchase or rental terms for equipment relating to accepting credit cards such as terminals and POS computer systems.

Chapter Seven

Summary

Have you discovered the secrets to beating sleazy, conniving credit card salespeople at this game? Through reading this book, you should now know more than most credit card salespeople out there. You should know that your rate is not determined entirely by the credit card processor, but by the type of card you accept for payment, by the way you take the card, and by the type of program your processor has put you on, Cost Plus or Tiered. You should now know that *no one can compare their rates with your current rates* unless they have accurate data on what kinds of cards you take and how many cards you take for each type of transaction.

The processor deserves to make money for his services like monitoring for fraud, reconciling your account, transferring monies from the networks to your bank account, troubleshooting technical problems, and handling vendor services and other customer service concerns. What is the value of that service to you?

Do you have a better understanding of how to figure the surcharge over the interchange rate that your processor is charging you? Do you receive an honest disclosure of fees with your monthly merchant statement? Are you armed and ready to hire someone you can trust, to hire someone who will answer the phone and be supportive when you have concerns? Or perhaps you really would prefer the lowest rates with 1-800-IGNORE-ME service. It is your choice and you are now educated in making that choice.

I hope you have gained the understanding I intended to convey to you through this book. I have added a bonus chapter which will serve to warn you of some of the tricks out there as well as hopefully entertain you a bit. This is a cut and dry subject, the old math class returned, so I have attempted to end with a little fun entertainment.

Go get the rates and the service you choose and deserve!

Gingergaye Hollowell
www.ElectronicMoneyCompany.com

Bonus Chapter

Bloody Stories Dealing with Bob from Brand X

Only Charging 1%

Bob is back at it again. Recently, Bob showed up at one of our clients' with a story that he was only going to charge the merchant 1%, and by the way, they needed all new equipment. The client called our office to ask for our review. It turns out Brand X was charging 1% *on top of* all the other qualified, mid-qualified, and non-qualified fees, but Bob neglected to explain that in his presentation. Another point he forgot to explain: there was a $995 early termination fee! Lord, have mercy! Does Bob have to trick people into signing up and then charge them for wanting to leave his bad service?

Huge Savings

Bob, Bob, Bob... what do you have going this time? Bob thought he was doing a comparison for a merchant. He wrote across the paper, "Savings: $800." The merchant asked us to take a look. "Where was the detailed comparison? Where was the savings of $800?" they asked. "Beats me. Why don't I just write $1,000 savings on a piece of paper," I replied. Bob, that is *not* a comparison. And you better learn how to list all the fees if you do learn how to do a proper comparison, not just some of them. How inconvenient for Bob to have to learn to understand the business he is in.

Rates on the App Were Different

We have a client who calls us once a year to review their types of transactions and see if they are running them properly to their best benefit. Turns out this year, Bob from Brand X had submitted his bid for their business. He had a proper letter outlining his proposed fees (turns out it was not a complete list).

He had pre-filled out an application with his rates. (Turns out Bob does not even know how to properly fill out an application. Turns out Bob put different figures on the application; higher ones.) Poor Bob. Will he ever get it right?

Horrible Swindle

One of our favorite salespeople called on a husband/wife merchant for credit card processing. They gave him a monthly statement to review, but were acting quite nervous. Our salesperson brought them back a comparison, explained all the fees, and showed them where we could save them money. They understood and acknowledged they wanted to save money, but they were absolutely scared to death to switch.

It turns out that they were so nervous because their previous salesperson, Bob from Brand X, had sold them some equipment on a lease for $39.95, but he secretly changed it to $89.95 after they had signed. They argued until they were blue in the face with the leasing company, but got nowhere because they hadn't saved a copy of the document they signed with Bob. We did end up lowering their rates and reprogramming their leased equipment. And of course, we left them a copy of everything they signed before leaving their store. But what a horrible thing to do to somebody, Bob!

Too Smart for His Own Britches

An acquaintance of mine started quizzing me one day on credit card machines and rates. A couple of weeks later, he was trying to sell me some equipment he had bought on EBay! Unbelievable! I, of course, said NO. Another couple of weeks later, he was asking me how to remove proprietary chips from the machines! He got burned buying equipment that couldn't be reprogrammed. I don't feel sorry for him.

Transaction Limit

One of our new clients told us this story about his experience with Bob from Brand X. He is a landscaper and needs to run one or two transactions per month, albeit they are large transactions. He was sold a wireless machine for a whopping $69 per month on a four-year lease. Then he had statement fees and minimum charges every month on top of his credit card fees. But here is the real kicker. The processor would only approve transactions under $300 and most of his transactions were way over that. So he was paying about $140 per month for nothing. Bob, why do you scam someone into signing up when you know all along your merchant cannot benefit from your service?

Neglected to Tell You about Interchange Rates

Bob has been busy in Alamogordo, NM. He is running around telling merchants that his company only charges 75 basis points. What he should be saying is that he charges interchange costs *plus* 75 basis points, which is kind of a high rate. Hope none of you are getting fooled by his new tricks. 0.75% sure sounds low, and that is because Bob is not telling you that it is added to the interchange and assessments.

Selling a New Equipment Lease

Fred has a car mechanic shop. When I stopped by to talk to him about his card processing, he brought out his bank statement and showed me that some charges were on his statement relating to his credit card processing. Poor Fred had switched processors a while back and got new equipment, but had never cancelled or paid off his old lease.

Now he was looking for an upgrade in equipment again, but he was still paying on not one lease, but two old leases! Bob from Brand X had sold him a new lease without explaining how to pay off the previous one. Fred had been paying on the first least for about eight years and the second lease for over four years. I was able to contact both leasing companies and get his payoff amount. He paid a bunch of dollars to move on.

Your Machine is Out of Date

This is a typical opener for Bob. But is your machine *really* out of date or does Bob just want to sell you a new machine or sign you up for an expensive new lease? Give us a call and double check Bob's story before you get suckered into a lease on a new machine when your current machine is working just fine for you and could last another year or two, maybe even longer.

I Forgot to Read What was in Front of Me

Bob from Brand X had written NO ETF (Early Termination Fee) near the signature line at a local car detail shop. But right above the signature line in the contract was the verbiage, "NO ALTERATIONS OR STRIKE-OUTS TO THE PROGRAM WILL BE ACCEPTED AND, IF MADE, ANY SUCH ALTERATIONS OR STRIKE-OUTS SHALL NOT APPLY." And higher up on the page was a paragraph, "The Agreement contains a provision that in the event you terminate the Agreement early, you will be responsible for the payment of early termination fees as set forth in Section 35." And of course, Section 35 was not available for reading.

Rate Guarantee

Bob's new quote sheet has a guarantee. Let's take a look.

"We will not increase the qualified discount rate for 48 months."

Response to Bob – BS.

How many cards are charged a qualified discount rate? Answer: not very many. Most cards today are debit cards and rewards cards, and then there are corporate cards, keyed-in cards… the list keeps going. Most processors have six tiers of rates. So if one rate tier is guaranteed to stay the same but the other five are not, the guarantee is worth "nuttin, honey."

Bob's qualified discount rate guarantee means absolutely nothing.

Is it Worth it to Switch?

Bob's favorite pitch still seems to be, "Let me do a comparison and I guarantee I'll save you money." Ask yourself if you want to save money if it is going to cost you more in other areas.

Do you want to go through the hassle of doing a comparison, which will be in hieroglyphics instead of English, to possibly only save a couple bucks? Do you want to give up the local service and support you now have? Do you want to change over to a company who uses technicians from China or India? Do you want to get locked into a long contract with a company and people you do not know or trust? Do you want to send your money to a company out of state? Do you want to get stuck in a contract with a HUGE termination fee if you later decide to leave their lousy service? Do you want to pad Bob's pocket with a commission when you will probably never see or hear from him again? Do you want to call 1-800-IGNORE-ME for service questions?

Isn't your time more valuable than to bother with a scammer like Bob?

Flat Rate

Bob's new trick is an old one. His new rate is 1.69% and he says he won't have any higher rates for keyed-in cards, rewards cards, or corporate cards (?). I think that Bob is either an outright liar or he is new to credit card processing and doesn't have a clue what he's talking about. Too bad the company he represents has such a high termination fee and some merchants will get sucked into an expensive learning experience.

I am proud that my industry has created PCI compliance and is requiring merchants to protect consumer's credit card numbers and information. But when is the industry going to police the processors whose salespeople give out fraudulent information to potential merchant customers? When will the industry require honest disclosure of fees? When will the industry protect the merchant from Bob?

"What a Whopper!"

Bob's got a new twist on his game and has been practicing it in Santa Fe, NM. He tells merchants that his rate is 1% and $0.00 for debit transactions. **What a Whopper!** (He doesn't tell them that the rates can go up after the first month.) In order to make a killer upfront commission, he signs the merchant up for a **non-cancellable** equipment lease of $180 per month for four years! Unbelievable! (This supposedly covers his losses on the rates.) He loses money on the rate for the first month **BUT** then the supercharged rates kick in. And the merchant is still stuck in the *ridiculous lease for equipment and a contract for card processing with a huge termination fee.*

Lesson: If it sounds too good to be true, it is *not real*! Be cautious and call us before you even think about signing anything. It is just too sad when someone gets bamboozled.

No PCI Compliance

Let's talk about PCI compliance. We have recently heard from a potential client that Bob from Brand X told them he didn't have a PCI compliance fee.

It just ain't so. PCI compliance is now *mandatory* for all processors. All processors have to pass on the cost of surveying merchants to make sure they understand how to protect cardholder data. PCI compliance is for everyone's benefit, cardholders *and* merchants.

We know of a restaurant that took all their credit card receipts and put them in a box. They put the box in their car to drive over to their bookkeeper's office. On the way, they stopped to get gas and the car was stolen, along with all the credit card information. The industry fined them two $50,000 fines! Needless to say, they had to close their business.

This happened a few years ago before we stopped printing the whole number on the receipts, but the idea is still the same. The fines are horrendous! So let's all get on the program. Even you, Bob.

The Bank is God

Sometimes Bob works for the bank. His boss, the bank, is interested in getting businesses to deposit their money. Merchant services are an add-on bonus for the bank. In reality, the bank outsources their merchant services and bumps up the margins in exchange for acting as a middleman. The bank doesn't really know or want to understand the industry, much less take the time to train Bob to understand the interchange costs and keep up with all the changes. As a result, many times Bob ends up misleading merchants and giving them incorrect or less than adequate information. The service is also outsourced with out-of-state technical support. The interchange rates and pricing of merchant services is a complicated and ever-changing business. The equipment side of the business is getting more complicated as well with the introduction of web gateways and mobile processing with smart phones.

Only $.10 for Debit

Bob is going around town telling people he can do debit transactions for $.10. What he is not telling people is all the other charges for debit. Each different network has different rates and transaction fees for their cost. He is adding $.10 onto those costs and perhaps onto some other non-disclosed fees. The problem is that some merchants still believe in fairy tales. Please be careful out there, folks. Beware of flying pigs.

Missing Close Letter

We have a client who switched over to us a few months ago. We heard from them last week that they are still having trouble cancelling their old merchant account. We explained that the best way to do that is in writing and by getting confirmation via fax machine that the fax was sent. We also advised her to keep a copy of that fax confirmation. Lo and behold, she explained to us that she had done all of that, multiple times even, and still her account was open and incurring monthly minimum fees. Unfortunately, we don't know what to advise someone who is getting stuck with fees from a dishonest company. Perhaps changing bank accounts is all we could come up with. We know that is a pain and yes, you would probably get a hit on your credit report, but that beats paying fees every month to a scam company. Of course, Bob is no longer in existence on the face of this earth to help her.

I Will Save You 50%

Recently a merchant told me how they had just switched their processing through Bob, who told them they were going to save 50% on their processing fees. Processors all work off the same cost, which is interchange. Interchange is the money the banks make for extending credit with the credit cards they issue. Visa and MasterCard add approximately a tenth of a percent on top of interchange. The processor makes another small sliver on top of that in order to service the merchant. Nobody, not even the scummiest of credit card salespeople on the planet, are marking up the costs 100%. In the case of 50% savings, Bob is misrepresenting the comparison in order to get the sale.

Our Rate is Only 1.49%

It is amazing to me how many new tricks there are to fool merchants into paying higher rates. Here is a new one. Give the retail swiped rate for personal credit cards below cost at 1.49% knowing full well that hardly any cards will come in at that rate. Then jack up the price for rewards cards, corporate cards, and even debit cards. Bob makes a bundle and the unsuspecting merchant pays the price.

I Only Charge You "COST"

Let's say Bob comes in and quotes you COST for all retail swiped personal credit cards. You're thinking, "Man this is great, I'm getting cost!" But the fact is that you only take one or two retail swiped personal credit cards each month. Most of your swiped cards are debit cards and Bob is now marking them up a ton. So Bob isn't saving you anything at all. He's actually charging you more. There are lots of ways to put lipstick on a pig!

"I'm With Your Credit Company" Fake Call

Here's a new gimmick from Bob. He calls a prospect and says that he is with their credit card processing company and noticed they were being overcharged for fees. If they send him the last two months' statements, he can work on a refund for them. It is all a lie.

Terminal Paper

I actually met a guy on a shuttle bus to a marketing seminar. Get this! His first job at 14 was with a telemarketing company that sold credit card terminal paper! He actually worked for and earned commissions selling $300 cases of paper for terminals to unsuspecting employees and owners. His script was to say he was with their credit card company and they knew they were low on paper, so could he ship them a case?! Don't talk to people who want to ship you credit card paper! Call us if you are not already on our gold service package for free paper.

Only Cost plus .20% Fake Out

New game plan from Bob hits the scene – quote the customer cost plus a low percentage like .20%, but don't tell the customer that debit cards, airline rewards cards, and corporate cards will be billed back at a higher rate than cost plus .20%, which most of the cards end up being! Hardly anyone ever receives just a plain old credit card anymore. Now the unsuspecting merchant thinks they are getting a killer deal, too good to be true. They don't stop to think that, at cost plus .20%, the processor is not making enough money to even begin to service the account. When they get their first statement, sometimes the new customer doesn't even bother to compare the new statement to their old processor's statement. Then two or three months go by and the customer decides to look at the statement to discover that they are paying even more than they were before. But lo and behold, calls to the processor go unanswered. And lo and behold again, there is the discovery of a huge termination fee. What is a customer to do? Discernment is the only answer.

New Terminal Lease Fake Out

Bob is still out there selling high leases on equipment. I ran across a merchant last week who was told she needed a new terminal for $100 lease payments, but not to worry because her savings were way higher than $100/month. Wowza! Bob earned a great up-front commission on that one.

And there was no documentation on the monthly savings, just a verbal comment that she would be saving a bunch.

Shopping the Internet for Rates Nightmare

Some people shop the internet for credit card rates. This is scary to me! The rate structures of card processing is like balancing a scale, with not just two buckets to compare, but about a hundred. There are so many different rates for different types of cards and it is just plain difficult, to say the least, to compare tiered pricing, to cost plus pricing, to cost plus pricing with bill back, to flat rate pricing, to flat rate pricing except for… and so on… and so on.

It is just way too complicated for merchants to actually compare. And then you have to be careful of maintenance fees, annual fees, extra weird-name fees, and of course, the, "We have no contract, but in the fine print you get charged $1,000 if you switch within three years," hidden in fine print fee. So in the end, don't forget about the value of local service and support. That could be worth far more than a difference of a few dollars in a rate comparison. That is our favorite part of our day! Hearing from our clients and helping solve a concern is the feeling good stuff that lets us know we are making a difference in someone's business success.

Wells Fargo Calling… NOT!

Recently a customer relayed a story about her previous processor, Bob. He prospected her on the phone and told her he represented Wells Fargo, which just happened to be her bank. He told her she would save money on her checking account fees if she used Wells Fargo credit card processing services. So she signed up. When she got the first statement, she discovered that her processor was *not* Wells Fargo, but some company out of state.

We Only Charge Interchange

Recently there was an article from our industry magazine about a processor selling interchange pricing. But it turned out they were padding the interchange and not disclosing this to their merchants. So the merchant was paying interchange plus a surcharge, all under a category called interchange.

Read the Fine Print

I recently spoke with a non-profit who closed one of their entities. They went to close their merchant services account at their bank, and lo and behold, they found out that the contract they had signed stated they would be responsible for paying the average surcharge fees the bank had been collecting from their merchant services until the end of the contract, even though they were not processing anymore! They certainly didn't understand that stipulation at the beginning of their agreement.

The Fake Flat Rate

I recently spoke with a new business wanting to set up credit card processing. He wanted to compare us to another company that gave him a quote with a flat rate of 1.89% and $.19. The rate was, obvious to me but not obvious to a rookie, only for qualified transactions. I knew it was too low for rewards cards, corporate cards, and keyed-in cards. At the quoted rate, the processor would lose money big time. The prospect didn't believe that he was being lied to, so I asked him to send me a copy of the application that they wanted him to sign. Of course, on the app was an extra 2.99% over the original 1.89%. When I pointed it out to him, he became a believer. Lesson: Don't trust verbal quotes and quotes in emails. Read the fine print on the agreement.

The PCI Trick

Today, one of our merchants called because they had received a phone call from someone saying they were with merchant services regarding their PCI compliance. The caller went on to explain that their machine was not PCI compliant and that he could send out a new one at no cost right away. Our merchant was wise and pushed to find out from the caller exactly who would cover the cost of the new machine. He finally admitted that he was from another processor and could give her a new machine if she switched. (New rates would cover the cost of a new machine.)

WOW! Sleazy Bob has lowered himself to a new even lower level of no integrity, trying to scare and trick merchants using PCI as a weapon. As I explained previously, terminals are required to be EMV chip ready by October, 2015, but this is *not* a PCI situation. No one has a terminal that is not PCI compliant, and PCI and EMV are two separate issues.

A Personal Afterword

In closing, I want to congratulate you for taking the time to educate yourself on this complicated subject. I am sure that you are now armed to negotiate with your current processor or to build a relationship with a new, trusted processor. In fact, I want to congratulate you for being an entrepreneurial spirit and building our country's economy with your small business.

I encourage you to keep following your passion, your desires, and your bliss. Earl Nightingale said, "We become what we think about most of the time." Napoleon Hill said, "Whatever the mind of man can conceive, and bring itself to believe, it can achieve." Find the gold in every moment, be happy, and take action! Continue to be an example of achievement.

Gingergaye Hollowell

Gingergaye Hollowell
www.ElectronicMoneyCompany.com

Addendum C

Interchange Switch Fees Cost Listing*

This information is confidential and proprietary of National Processing Company.

Chargetypes			New Interchange		Switch Fees
FNBO	BuyPass	Interchange Category	%	$	$
1800	1970	Interlink	0.75%	0.170	0.0350
1801	1971	Interlink Supermarket	0.00%	0.250	0.0350
1803	1903	Interlink Fuel	0.70%	0.170	0.0350
1804	1904	Interlink Fuel Maximum	0.00%	0.950	0.0350
1806	1906	Maestro Supermarket/Whse Max	0.00%	0.350	0.0250
1810	1972	Maestro	0.90%	0.150	0.0250
1813	1927	Maestro Supermarket/Whse	1.05%	0.150	0.0250
1814	1928	Maestro Convenience Stores	0.75%	0.170	0.0250
1816	1930	Maestro Convenience Stores Max	0.00%	0.950	0.0250
1820	1973	Star	0.75%	0.160	0.0425
1851	1951	Star Medical - Trans < $15.00	1.20%	0.060	0.0425
1820	1973	Star Medical - Trans > $15.01	0.75%	0.160	0.0425
1852	1952	Star Small Ticket Retail < $10.00	1.25%	0.060	0.0425
1820	1973	Star Small Ticket Retail > $10.01	0.75%	0.160	0.0425
1821	1931	Star Maximum	0.00%	0.660	0.0425
1822	1932	Star Grocery	0.00%	0.250	0.0425
1823	1933	Star QSR	1.25%	0.040	0.0425
1853	1953	Star QSR Maximum	0.00%	0.460	0.0425
1824	1920	Star Petroleum	0.80%	0.140	0.0425
1826	1922	Star Petroleum Maximum	0.00%	0.710	0.0425
1835	1976	NYCE	0.75%	0.150	0.0425
1830	1915	NYCE Other Minimum	0.00%	0.260	0.0425
1831	1916	NYCE Petroleum	0.85%	0.150	0.0425
1832	1917	NYCE Petroleum Maximum	0.00%	0.260	0.0425
1833	1918	NYCE QSR Minimum	0.00%	0.185	0.0425
1836	1934	NYCE Grocery	0.00%	0.260	0.0425
1837	1935	NYCE QSR	0.55%	0.065	0.0425
1838	1936	NYCE QSR Maximum	0.00%	0.500	0.0425
1840	1977	Pulse Retail	0.74%	0.100	0.0700
1843	1943	Pulse Grocery	0.00%	0.215	0.0700
1844	1944	Pulse Petroleum	0.74%	0.100	0.0700
1845	1978	Accel	75.00%	0.150	0.0300
1847	1938	Accel Grocery	0.00%	0.250	0.0300
1848	1948	Accel QSR	1.25%	0.030	0.0300
1849	1949	Accel QSR Maximum	0.00%	0.450	0.0300
1855	1980	Shazam	0.75%	0.150	0.0400
1856	1939	Shazam Grocery	0.00%	0.210	0.0400
1858	1958	Shazam Petroleum	0.75%	0.130	0.0400
1865	1965	Shazam QSR	1.25%	0.050	0.0400
1867	1967	Shazam Small Ticket < $25.00	1.25%	0.050	0.0400
1875	1984	AFFN	0.65%	0.120	0.0300
1876	1986	AFFN Maximum	0.00%	0.500	0.0300
1877	1987	AFFN Major Merchants	0.50%	0.065	0.0300
1878	1988	AFFN Major Merchants Maximum	0.00%	0.400	0.0300
1879	1989	AFFN Supermarket	0.00%	0.170	0.0300
1805	1905	Alaska Option	0.00%	0.260	-
1899		Debit Unknown	0.00%	0.340	-
	1985	Debit Unknown	0.00%	0.375	-

*Rates as of November 2009. Subject to change from time to time by the Debit Networks.

What Merchant Clients Are Saying About Electronic Money Company

"You came in and rescued us from the current provider that we were with and about to lose customers over, and you rescued those customers from that high priced product and allowed us to keep and maintain those customers at our bank. You turned a cost center into a profit center. We are confident in referring our customers to you for their merchant services because we know that your support to us and prompt customer service to our clients has not only kept the current customers with our bank, but also helped bring new customers into our bank."

–Sean Ormand, President, 1st New Mexico Bank of Silver City, NM

"On behalf of us here at Beaver Toyota, I would just like to tell you thanks a million for your great service. I know that we were with your company prior to this last time but had switched over to Elavon. Due to the inconsistency of promises that were made in regard to lower pricing and settings on our machines, we have cancelled our other contract. We are pleased to let you know that you have met all of our requests and will continue to conduct business with you and your company."

–Kelly Clark, Beaver Toyota, Santa Fe, NM

"I had 3 different processors before I found Electronic Money Company. The other processors never did what they said they were going to do. They took out a bunch of hidden fees they hadn't told me about. EMC always did what they said. They were straight-forward and honest. I knew exactly what fees they were going to take out and why. There were no unexpected surprises!"

–Deiadra Phelps, Soap and Spa Essentials, Albuquerque

"I am so happy to be back with your credit card processing and I am so sorry I let some stranger snow me with promises he didn't keep. I really missed your customer service and my bookkeeper is thrilled also because the statement is easier to reconcile."

–Char De Vasquez, Char Designer Suedes and Leathers, Santa Fe, NM since 1976

"The things that I like about Electronic Money Company are that the service is prompt and courteous. I have needed that service a couple times per year. The switch over to EMC was timely and good, and the expenses were less than the other company."

–Frank Basset, Owner, Wingbasket and New Mexico Pinon Coffee, Albuquerque, NM

"After ten years with the same processor, I listened to Electronic Money Company (EMC). They demonstrated my potential credit card processing savings based upon my numbers. Within 24 hours the system was running and processing credit cards without a problem. I immediately started saving on the credit card charges.

"The support is excellent. No more lost charges because of malfunctioning credit card machines. Thank you for a great service."

–Kathleen M. O'Connor, Esq. and Incoming President of CP Cal, Pasadena, CA

"I have been with Electronic Money Company for over six years. Other processors call me all the time but I tell them I will not change. My sales rep takes the time to come to my place of business and explain to me all the charges in detail and how to keep my rates low. Every time I call, she is always helpful and gets back to me right away."

–Christian Dimery, Owner, Morningside Antiques, Albuquerque, NM

"I accept large purchasing cards in my business. I saved over $900 last month on my card processing! EMC is amazing! And the secret turned out to be so simple!"

–Mike Rode, Dynamic Communications, Albuquerque, NM

"I am thrilled to find a company that actually provides hands-on live support to their customers. Carolyn, the office manager for Electronic Money Company, is a great help in straightening out issues, and after being neglected for over two years by my former company. Thanks so much."

–Jake Finkelstein, Spectrum Auction LLC, Placitas, NM

"We were talked into moving our business away from Electronic Money Company by our bank. We made the move and discovered that the rate they charged was higher than our rate with EMC. We also did not receive the personal service and attention everyone at EMC has always given us. We are very pleased to be back in such good hands, not to mention we are saving money."

–Chuck and Sharon Lutheran, Owners, The Mechanic Inc., Albuquerque, NM

"Electronic Money Company has been working with us now for three years plus and has done a phenomenal job of dealing with us on any of our concerns, issues, and handling of our equipment. I would highly recommend them for any merchant service or equipment. We get several calls per week from other credit card processors that are pushy and demanding, only wanting to scam us, saying they are going to save us money. I have told my employees that flat out we don't want to change because of the service we get from Electronic Money Company. There aren't too many honest credit card processors like them anymore, that you can trust you're getting the honest truth about all the 'hidden fees.'"

–Tom Coughlin, Owner, Tom's RV Service and Sales, Albuquerque, NM

"We have been using Electronic Money Company at our hotels for three years. After using their services, I was impressed with their customer service and the responsiveness to our needs. They are willing to work with large groups of businesses to give the best processing rates possible. With the rates we have received, we have no need to consider another processing company for our hotels. All our hotels are using Electronic Money Company: Hampton Inn, Holiday Inn Express Hotel & Suites, Days Inn, and Comfort Suites. We are pleased to have local representation for our properties."

–Pete Desai, Owner, Hampton Inn, Alamogordo, NM

About the Author

Gingergaye and her husband, Walt, have raised 8 children together, 4 boys and 4 girls.

She has been an entrepreneur since the year 2000 when she started her business, Electronic Money Company Inc., providing credit card processing and other small business services such as business mobile apps, business analytic tools, and Point of Sale Systems. Now she carries on her nurturing through her family of clients.

She wrote this book after being sick and tired of hearing all the horror stories from so many clients who had been duped by "Bob from Brand X" into thinking they were going to get better rates on their card processing, when in fact they were charged more and locked into contracts! Connect with Gingergaye at www.ElectronicMoneyCompany.com.

www.ingramcontent.com/pod-product-compliance
Lightning Source LLC
Chambersburg PA
CBHW051731170526
45167CB00002B/896